At the Sign of
"The Crippled Harlequin"

A thriller

Norman Robbins

Samuel French — London
www.samuelfrench-london.co.uk

CHARACTERS

Marjory Pike, seventies
Sally Lockwood, thirties
Pamela Seton, forties
Bryan Lockwood, thirties
Joan Reece, thirties
Derek Tyndale, early forties
Lionel Reece, fifties
Isobel Clarke, late twenties

SYNOPSIS OF SCENES

The action of the play takes place in the lounge of "Peak Lodge", a small guest-house in Derbyshire's Peak District

ACT I
SCENE 1   A late afternoon in December. A few days
            before Christmas
SCENE 2   An hour later

ACT II
SCENE 1   Three hours later
SCENE 2   Two hours later

Time — the present

Other plays and pantomimes by
Norman Robbins
published by Samuel French Ltd

Aladdin
Ali Baba and the Forty Thieves
Babes in the Wood
Cinderella
Dick Whittington
The Grand Old Duke of York
Hansel and Gretel
Hickory Dickory Dock
Humpty Dumpty
Jack and Jill
Jack and the Beanstalk
The Late Mrs Early
Nightmare
The Old Woman Who Lived in a Shoe
Pull the Other One
Puss in Boots
Red Riding Hood
Rumpelstiltzkin
Sing a Song of Sixpence
Slaughterhouse
Sleeping Beauty
Snow White
Tiptoe Through the Tombstones
Tom, the Piper's Son
A Tomb with a View
Wedding of the Year
The White Cat
The Wonderful Story of Mother Goose

For Jean and Dennis Canning
who love the theatre

ACT I
Scene 1

The lounge of "Peak Lodge", a small guest-house near Edale in the Peak District. A few days before Christmas

The only entrance to the lounge is UR and boasts a rarely-closed glazed door which opens on to the rear wall of the room. A glimpse of the main entrance hall may be afforded through the opening, but this is by no means essential. DS of the door is a small bookcase containing a selection of paperback novels and magazines. On top of this is a ceramic bowl filled with decorated pine-cones topped with a sprig of red-berried holly. To each side of the bowl, Christmas greetings cards stand. DS of this, the original fireplace has been removed and a boxed-in radiator occupies the space. Various small ornaments cover its surface. Above this a heavy-framed eighteenth-century oil painting or print of the original building, blackened with age, is fixed to the wall and, above this, a lighting fitment to illuminate it. In a recess DS of the chimney breast is a television set, angled US so that the screen cannot be seen by the audience, with, beside it, a magazine rack containing various magazines.

In the rear wall, deeply recessed, are two tall and wide windows separated by a long coffee table, topped with an impressive artificial Christmas tree, heavily laden with lights, globes, tinsel, etc. Gaily-wrapped boxes and packages are beneath it. Both windows have wide ledges on which ceramic bowls of hyacinths are flanked by ornamental globes left over from the tree. Fake snow has been applied to the panes of glass within each recess, but glimpses of the spectacular countryside can still be seen. A comfortable window seat is below each window and is framed by thick, swagged drapes and matching pelmets. In the wall L, and opposite the radiator, is a very large window with drapes and pelmet to match the others. This too is decorated with fake snow. A tall vase of holly sprigs and mistletoe occupies the centre of the ledge, and is flanked by copper or brass bowls filled with Christmas globes and tinsel

US of the window is an oblong oak table, angled towards the radiator. Three upright chairs are arranged at this, one with its back to the corner of the room and the other two on the short side, L and R. DS of the window is a small writing desk topped by a small table lamp and various Christmas cards. Above the desk there is a framed theatrical poster, circa 1895. A fourth upright chair is at the desk. Its back to the bookcase, angled C, is a comfortable-looking

*armchair. A matching settee is just off C of the room, a copy of the "TV Times"
on the US arm, and DL is another armchair. All have bright cushions for extra
comfort and appeal. Behind the settee is a drop-wing table and on top of this,
a tray holding a small teapot, milk jug, sugar bowl, spoon and a used cup and
saucer. The room is thickly carpeted and the walls are dotted with assorted
prints and paintings, each decorated with sprigs of holly or mistletoe. The
rest of the room is brightly trimmed with Christmas decorations*

When the CURTAIN *rises, it is a dull afternoon. The overhead lights are dim
so, apart from the twinkling lights on the tree, the room looks cheerless*

*Marjory Pike, a frail-looking but elegant woman in her seventies, is sitting
in the armchair L, writing postcards*

*After a moment, Sally Lockwood, a pleasant and comfortably-dressed
woman in her early thirties, enters and crosses to the table behind the settee
to collect the tray. She sees Marjory with surprise*

Sally Mrs Pike. I thought you were out.
Marjory (*looking up*) Oh, yes. I was. But didn't get far, I'm afraid. Only
down to the stepping stones. (*Giving a little laugh*) Mr Tyndale was right.
They're almost covered. Much too dangerous to risk a crossing.
Sally (*grimacing*) Last night's rain, I expect. Didn't ease off till after three.
But you could have followed the path and crossed lower down. There *is* a
footbridge. I told Bryan to mention it.
Marjory (*quickly*) Oh, he did, Mrs Lockwood. He was *most* helpful. But to
tell you the truth I didn't like the look of the sky, and the wind was much
sharper than I expected. I really needed a warmer coat. "Marjory," I
thought, "there's no point in being silly. You'll be far better off in the
comfort of *Peak Lodge* writing your cards." So before I could change my
mind, I turned round and made my way back again. (*Anxiously*) It is all
right? You don't mind my being here?
Sally Of course not. But you shouldn't be straining your eyes in *this* light.
(*She moves back to the door and flicks up an unseen switch in the hall*)

*The overhead lights come up to full. From this point on, the exterior lights
fade as night falls*

That's better. You can see what you're doing now. (*She returns to the tray
and picks it up*) Is there anything I can get for you? A cup of tea? Glass of
sherry?
Marjory (*gratefully*) I wouldn't say no to the tea. (*Hastily*) But not if it's any
trouble.

Deer

HAD TO REOPEN THIS AS I
SEALED IT WITHOUT WRITING
THE MESSAGE. OOPS! JE.

Sally (*shaking her head with a smile*) We usually have one ourselves about this time, so Bryan'll have the kettle on. (*After a hesitation*) Now you're sure you're warm enough? I *can* turn the heating up.

Marjory (*quickly*) Oh, no. I'm fine, thank you. Warm as toast. (*After a hesitation*) Well ... perhaps *a teensy* bit warmer would be nice.

Sally (*smiling*) I thought so. (*She puts the tray down again and moves to the boxed-in radiator*) It's often quite chilly by mid-afternoon at this time of year, but if no-one's about, we turn it down to keep the bills more manageable. (*She adjusts the knob*)

Marjory (*guiltily*) Oh, I didn't mean ...

Sally No, no. Don't worry. I should think they'll *all* be making their way back by this time, and we don't want them freezing to death before dinner. (*She goes back to collect the tray*) It'd be a waste of good food.

Marjory (*shyly*) I must say I'm looking forward to it. Lunch was delicious.

Sally (*lifting the tray*) One of Bryan's recipes. (*Confidentially*) Top secret and coveted by cooks the world over. (*Drily*) So he *tells* me. Been in his family for *centuries*. Well — maybe the nineteen-forties. (*She laughs*)

Marjory (*smiling*) And what's on the menu tonight? Or mayn't I ask?

Sally (*lowering the tray again*) Soup *Lorraine,* that's chicken and almonds with a blend of spices. Rack of lamb, or baked salmon. The usual selection of veg, and Grandma Lockwood's apple tansy or clementine and chocolate pudding to follow. Plus the cheese board, of course.

Marjory (*raising an eyebrow*) No Bakewell tart?

Sally (*in mock shock*) Mrs *Pike*. Bakewell *pudding,* if you *don't* mind. The locals would hang you for calling it a tart. (*Amused*) It's the first thing I learned when we moved here. (*In snooty tones*) "We don't have tarts in Bakewell, Mrs Lockwood. The correct term is *puddings*." (*She laughs*) I can arrange one for tomorrow, if you'd like? It's sometimes on the menu in tourist season, but not as often in winter.

Marjory (*smiling*) There's no need. Really, there isn't. I only mentioned it because we're so close to Bakewell and thought there'd be some connection.

Sally (*nodding*) Invented by a cook at the *Rutland Arms*. Some time in the eighteen-hundreds. A pure accident, according to local legend, but the famous Jane Austen raved about it, so everyone jumped on the bandwagon. You'll have to try one before you go home. The ones you buy in supermarkets aren't a patch on the genuine article. (*She picks up the tray*) I'll get you that tea.

Sally exits

(*Off*) Cup of tea, Pammy? You look as though you could use one.

Marjory goes back to her postcard writing

Pamela (*off*) Tell me about it. It's colder than a witch's *you-know-what*. Just give me a chance to shed this and I'll be right with you.
Sally (*off*)Two minutes. In the lounge.

Pamela Seton enters the lounge unfastening her bulky jacket. She is forty or so, with a positive, almost masculine attitude, wearing a woollen cap, jeans, thick sweater, stout walking shoes and a bright red knitted scarf. She moves to the radiator, glancing at Marjory as she does so

Pamela (*brightly*) You've more sense than I have. (*She presses her hands to the radiator*)
Marjory (*looking up*) I'm sorry?
Pamela It's freezing out there. There'll be six foot of snow by tomorrow.
Marjory (*glancing at the window in dismay*) Oh, dear.
Pamela (*hastily*) Only joking. But if you do see three brass monkeys hanging around, you'll know what they're looking for. (*She laughs*) I'm Pam, by the way. Pam Seton. Though mostly I answer to Pammy.
Marjory (*introducing herself*) Marjory Pike.
Pamela (*slipping her jacket off*) Arrived last night, did you?
Marjory (*apologetically*) Well after nine, I'm afraid.
Pamela Late start? Or just a long journey? (*She drapes her jacket on the back of the armchair and adds her scarf to it*)
Marjory All the way from London.
Pamela (*moving to the settee and removing her cap*) Sheffield's *my* base. I'm English and Drama at North Lane Community. (*She sits and tosses the cap on to the armchair*) Godawful place, but the head's decent enough and the kids seem to like me, so I shouldn't complain. (*Loosening her boot laces*) Been here before, have you?
Marjory To the lodge or Derbyshire?
Pamela (*still occupied*) Oh. Lodge.
Marjory (*shaking her head*) First visit. But I did visit Buxton once. Just after the war. (*Smiling*) We had an aunt who ran a tea-room there.
Pamela (*leaning back*) Umpteenth time for me. Four times a year, at least, for the past five. (*She grins*) As you'll have noticed, I like my walking and Derbyshire's walkers' heaven. The minute breakfast's out of the way, I'm into the wilds with a pack of sandwiches and a large flask of coffee. Forget civilization. Give me the peace and quiet of countryside any time. How'd you get to hear of it?
Marjory Through a friend. "Marjory," she said, "You'll love it. Pack a suitcase and book yourself in for a month. You'll never regret it."
Pamela (*enviously*) So you're here till the end of January?
Marjory (*amused*) Oh, no. No. Just over Christmas. I have to be back in London for New Year. But I'm sending her a postcard to let her know I've

arrived safely. (*She shows Pamela the card*) It's no use trying to telephone. She's been totally deaf for the past few years.

Pamela So what do you think of it? (*She indicates the room*) *Peak Lodge*?

Marjory (*smiling*) It's early days yet, but at the moment I'm enjoying it immensely.

Pamela Well, don't forget to put your name down for the panto party.

Marjory looks blank

(*Explaining*) At Buxton Opera House. Bryan and Sally arrange a trip every Boxing Day. (*Explaining*) Because of the *connection*.

Marjory continues to look puzzled

Jemmy *Junkins*.

The postcard slips from Marjory's hand

(*Realizing*) Sorry. Probably means nothing to *you*, but he's been one of *my* pet hobby-horses for years. (*Explaining*) He was one of the last *Harlequins* in the Drury Lane pantomimes and died in 1908. Worked with Dan Leno and Marie Lloyd, et cetera and did a Royal Command at Windsor Castle in 1895.

Marjory (*realizing the card is missing*) A little before my time, I'm afraid. (*She smiles and picks up the card again*)

Pamela (*laughing*) Mine too. But he popped up in one of the A level texts a few years ago and curiosity brought me down here. It's where he lived, you see? After his accident. He was doing his thing in *Red Riding Hood* at the Opera House in 1903 and broke his back falling through an open trapdoor.

Marjory (*wincing*) How *awful*.

Pamela (*nodding*) Only twenty-eight, and never walked again. No insurance, of course. Didn't have it in those days. But the management held a benefit night for him and raised enough cash to cover medical treatment and transport him here when he left the infirmary.

Marjory (*glancing around*) So this is where he lived?

Pamela Only for the *last* part of his life. He was a London boy, was Jemmy. And it wasn't a house *then*. It was an old coaching inn. *The Flying Horse*. (*She indicates the print on the wall*) That's a print of the original building. You can just make out the sign if you examine it under a glass. His younger brother, *Victor*, was the one who owned it — and wasn't exactly happy to be lumbered with a bedridden sibling. If it hadn't been for Jemmy's friends and the odd cheque or two, he'd have packed him off to the workhouse. As it was, he had the name changed to *The Crippled Harlequin* so no-one could forget *he* was his brother's main supporter, and Jemmy spent his last few years upstairs relying on "the kindness of strangers" as Tennessee Williams once put it. He was thirty-three when he died and hadn't a penny to his name.

Marjory (*shaking her head sadly*) Poor man.

Pamela There was almost a riot when people heard he'd been buried in a pauper's grave. Marie Lloyd sent money for a headstone, but it never materialized. Little brother cried abject poverty and claimed he'd used it to pay off part of Jemmy's debts, so the only marker ever set up was a wooden cross donated by a local carpenter. (*Disgustedly*) Even that's gone now, so it's pure guesswork where the grave actually is.

Marjory How very sad.

Pamela It'd be nice to think the old miser finally got what he deserved. But no. He lived here till 1949 and died worth *thousands*. Though *how* he did it, they hadn't a clue. It certainly wasn't from "passing trade" and most of the locals wouldn't give him the time of day. Not after Jemmy died. (*Thoughtfully*) Black marketing's *my* opinion. Some of them made a fortune from it during the war — but *you'll* probably know more about that than I do.

Marjory looks startled

(*Realizing*) I mean — I was only a twinkle in Daddy's eye at the time. But they never pinned anything on Victor, so if he *was* up to something nefarious, he managed to get away with it. Anyway — he'd no family and hadn't made a will, so His Majesty's Government copped the lot. After that, it was one owner after another. None of them stayed long, and most of 'em were gone inside a year. They kept the name though. It was still *The Crippled Harlequin* up to fifteen years ago — then a Manchester couple turned it into a guest house and christened it with the inspiring appellation of *Mon Repose*. (*She rolls her eyes*)

Marjory (*frowning*) I'm surprised they got permission.

Pamela (*shrugging*) It wasn't a listed building — though it should have been in *my* opinion — so legally there was nothing to stop them. Everything of historical or architectural interest went into the skip and the great god "contemporary" moved in.

Marjory (*puzzled*) But surely the landing window's original?

Pamela The stained-glass one, you mean? (*She shakes her head*) Looks authentic, I know, but it's only a repro. After the Manchester lot gave up and moved on, a local businessman had a go at restoring the place and that's one of his efforts. Spent a fortune, from all accounts, but it didn't improve trade. He sold to a Scottish couple — the Gregorys — the following year and they changed the name again and had "For Sale" notices up before the paint had time to dry. It had four more owners before the Lockwoods bought it in 2001.

Marjory So the Gregorys named it Peak Lodge?

Pamela (*shaking her head*) It was *Cairngorms* in their day. This one's down to the Lockwoods. They wanted to re-name it when they took over and Bryan found the old inn-sign in what was left of the stables. Would you believe some idiot had used it to board up a broken window? Anyway — after hearing about the place's history, they thought *The Crippled Harlequin Guest House* would appeal more to punters than *Cairngorms* ever did. But what they hadn't counted on was our old friend political correctness. When they tried to register the new name, the board turned it down on the grounds that some people might find it offensive and suggested *Peak Lodge* was a far more appropriate title. (*Grimacing*) So that's what it became. *Peak Lodge.*

Marjory (*interested*) Do they still have the sign?

Pamela Oh, yes. They've had it restored. It's up in their own room. If you'd like to see it, have a word with Sal. She'd be only too pleased.

Bryan Lockwood enters. He is a cheery thirty-something man in slacks, shirt, and thick sweater with pushed-up sleeves. He carries a tray holding a small china tea-pot, milk jug, sugar bowl, two cups and saucers, and two teaspoons

Bryan Here we are, ladies. Tea up. (*He deposits the tray on the table behind the settee*) Sorry it's taken so long. Sal got called to the phone. (*To Pamela*) Good walk today, Pammy? (*He picks up the "TVTimes" and moves down to the magazine rack*)

Pamela (*lightly*) Aren't they always? I was just telling Mrs Pike about the panto trip.

Bryan Oh, yes. (*He replaces the magazine and turns to Marjory*) You *will* be joining us, won't you? It's Boxing Day night and just a bit of fun.

Marjory (*protesting faintly*) I don't think …

Bryan (*quickly*) It's our treat. No charge. It's a kind of Christmas present to the guests for supporting us. (*Grinning*) Gives *us* a night out, too.

Marjory (*surprised*) That's very generous.

Bryan We get tickets as soon as booking starts. Can't have old Jemmy thinking we've forgotten him. He might start haunting again and frighten off the customers. (*He laughs and moves back* US)

Pamela He's welcome to haunt my room. I'd swap my ex for him any day.

Marjory (*amused*) I didn't know the lodge was haunted, Mr Lockwood.

Bryan (*smiling*) It's not. (*In a Scottish accent*) Nary a ghostly wail's disturbed us since the day we moved in.

Marjory But you said "again". He might start haunting again.

Bryan (*amused*) Just an old wives' tale. Who believes in ghosts these days? (*He picks up the teapot*) Shall I pour, or will you do it yourselves?

Marjory (*indicating for him to do it*) Please.

Pamela But it's why it changed hands so often, isn't it? After Victor died.

Bryan (*pouring tea*) According to the locals. But it was more likely bad management and gossip. (*Scornfully*) Clanking pipes, creaking floorboards and suddenly the place is knee deep in spooky visitors. Wooooooo. (*He laughs*) You don't have to worry, Mrs Pike. I promise we're a ghost-free establishment.

Marjory (*with mock regret*) Oh, dear — you've really spoilt my Christmas now. They're never the same without a ghost.

Bryan (*lightly*) The only one you'll see round here's the one in the pantomime. (*He moves down to Marjory carrying a cup and saucer, a spoon and the sugar bowl*) Unless, of course, you *really* feel deprived and in that case, for a small extra charge, I'll moan and groan outside your bedroom, Christmas Eve, rattling snow-chains till you beg for mercy.

Marjory (*taking the cup and saucer; amused*) That's *very* kind of you, Mr Lockwood, but I wouldn't want to put you out. (*She adds a spoonful of sugar to her tea*)

Bryan (*smiling*) It's no trouble. All part of the *Peak Lodge* service. (*He moves back to the tea-tray*) And it's Bryan.

Pamela But it was why the last owners sold, wasn't it? Because of Jemmy? They even called in an exorcist.

Bryan (*handing a cup to Pamela from the back of the settee; amused*) Where did you get *that* from?

Pamela (*surprised*) You told me. The first year you were here.

Bryan (*lightly*) I must have been pulling your leg.

Pamela (*protesting*) No, you weren't. You were tickled pink because it hadn't worked and they'd dropped the asking price by ten thousand pounds to get the place off their hands, I remember it, clear as day. (*She sips at her tea*)

Bryan (*laughing*) You've a better memory than I have. If I owned a so-called haunted house and wanted to get rid of it, I wouldn't drop the price. I'd double it and advertise to every crack-pot in the country. It'd be gone inside a week.

Sally enters

Sally That was the Tysons. They've had to cancel.

Bryan (*dismayed*) Not *again*.

Sally He's back in hospital. (*Wincing*) It doesn't sound good.

Bryan You're right. It leaves us with an empty room for Christmas.

Sally Well I'm sure he's not done it on purpose.

Bryan I know that. But we've been turning people away for weeks.

Sally (*soothingly*) There's always the chance of a last-minute booking. I'll give the information bureau a ring.

Bryan (*shaking his head*) It's all right. I'll call in tomorrow when I pick up the order from Millsons. (*He remembers something*) Which reminds me. I need to check that last invoice of theirs. I'm sure they've undercharged for the sirloin. It's not been that price since the nineteen-nineties. Better do it now before I forget again. (*He gives the others a quick smile*) 'Scuse me, ladies. Duty calls.

Bryan exits

Sally (*to the others*) Sorry about that. We don't usually discuss problems in public.

Pamela (*sympathetically*) Must be annoying, though. Being let down *this* close to Christmas. It's not the Nottingham couple, is it? Something to do with the BBC?

Sally (*remembering*) The Dysons, you mean? No, no. We've not seen them in months. They're visiting friends in New Zealand. (*Glancing round*) There's a card here, somewhere. (*Giving up*) No. These are the *Tysons*. Nice couple. Americans. About your age. They were here in May and booked again for October, but the husband was rushed into hospital the night before they were due to fly and had to cancel.

Marjory Oh, dear.

Sally It was touch and go for a few weeks, but the minute he came out, they gave us a call and re-booked for Christmas. And now it's happened again.

Pamela (*curiously*) So what's wrong with him?

Sally Something to do with his liver. Recurrent tumours, I think. She was pretty upset about it. (*Grimacing*) Some people have awful luck.

Marjory (*kindly*) He'll be in the best hands. The doctors there are very good.

Sally (*sighing*) I suppose so. But it's not surprising he had depression. It'd depress *me* being in and out of hospital every few months.

Pamela (*frowning*) Hm?

Sally (*shrugging*) He was taking pills for it. Narfil or Nardil. Something of the kind. Nothing I'd ever heard of. But it's on the bottle. He left them behind when they went and didn't realize till they'd reached the airport. I offered to post them, but he said if we'd keep them safe, he'd pick them up on their next visit. Which, of course, never happened.

Pamela So what are you going to do with them?

Sally (*helplessly*) Haven't a clue. They could have gone off, for all I know. I presume there's a sell-by date?

Marjory They do say unwanted medicines should be taken to the local chemist's.

Sally (*frowning*) I should have asked when I spoke to her, but never gave it a thought. Do you think I should call her back?

Pamela Well it's not as if he'll need them, is it? I mean — he's obviously not been without for the past few months. He could even have forgotten you've got them. I shouldn't worry about it. Drop 'em in at Boots.

Sally She might call when Christmas is over. She did say she'd let us know. (*Resolving the problem*) Oh, they can stay where they are. It's not as though we're tripping over them, is it? And they're safe enough in the first aid box. Are you all right for tea?

Marjory and Pamela smile and nod

Well, give me a call if you need anything.

Sally exits

Pamela (*finishing her tea and rising*) And I'll be off, as well. (*She moves behind the settee and puts her cup and saucer on the tray*) A long hot soak before dinner, then a few chapters of Katherine Hardy and an early night. (*She gathers up her belongings*) I'll see you in the dining room.

Lionel (*angry; off*) Well don't blame me. I didn't choose the bloody things.

Joan (*angry; off*) No. And you didn't tell me we'd be stuck in the middle of nowhere for Christmas, did you?

Pamela (*to Marjory; warningly*) The Reeces.

Lionel (*off*) And where do you think you find country guest-houses? The middle of flaming Rochdale?

Joan (*off*) When I said a country guest-house, I meant one with a road leading to it. Not half-way up a dirt track. Look at these shoes.

Lionel (*off*) The last thing that interests me now is your bloody shoes. If you bought ones the right size occasionally, you'd be a damned sight better off.

Joan (*off*) Oh, yes? You're an expert on women's shoes, as well, are you? Well for your information, Lionel Reece ... (*Sharply*) Where are you going?

Lionel (*off*) Upstairs.

Joan (*off*) And how do *I* get up there with my foot like this. What am *I* supposed to do?

Lionel (*off*) Limp.

Joan (*off*) Well, thank you very much. I'll remember that the next time you break a leg. (*Yelling*) And it can't be too damn soon.

Joan Reece limps into the room, face flushed with anger. She is a sullen and over-painted woman of thirty or so, wearing a full-length fur coat over expensive-looking clothes with matching accessories — including a handbag — and lots of flashy jewellery

Pamela (*with malicious sweetness*) Nice trip out, Mrs Reece?

Joan (*tartly*) If you call being frog-marched round godforsaken towns without a decent shop to their names "nice", it's been great. I've had more fun in a graveyard. (*She limps past Pamela to the* R *of the settee*)

Pamela (*smiling*) Yes. We have heard the rumours.

Joan glares at Pamela

Marjory (*sympathetically*) Not a country girl, I take it?

Joan (*balefully*) As far as I'm concerned, they can stick the countryside where the monkey sticks its nuts. (*She sits on the settee arm and massages her ankle*)

Pamela (*drily*) Such wonderful phraseology. You'd have turned him green with envy.

Joan (*frowning*) Who?

Pamela William Shakespeare.

Pamela exits

Joan looks baffled

Marjory (*brightly*) I'm rather fond of the country, myself, but my late sister would certainly have taken your side. Even as children we ——

Joan (*suddenly focusing on her*) Do I know you?

Marjory (*confused*) I'm sorry?

Joan (*impatiently*) Haven't we met before? You look familiar.

Marjory I don't think so. I only arrived last night. (*Quickly*) Marjory Pike.

Joan (*after a moment*) Joan Reece ... (*Darkly*) For the time being. (*She slips her shoe off with a theatrical gasp of relief*)

Marjory (*sympathetically*) New shoes?

Joan They were. (*Bitterly*) First time I get a chance to wear them and it has to be a bloody route march. (*She fingers her heel*) Sod it. Now I've got a blister.

Marjory (*smiling*) They've no idea, have they? Men.

Joan (*balefully*) That one certainly hasn't. I could wear clogs for all he'd care. Ninety-six pounds I paid for these and now look at 'em. (*She glares at her shoe*)

Marjory (*soothingly*) I'm sure they'll clean up.

Joan Not unless they do it themselves. I wear nothing unless it's immaculate. There's no make-do-and-mend about me. If you've got the brass, you let 'em know you have and spend it accordingly. I learned that in me teens. Nob'dy looks down their nose at Joanie Claythorpe. (*Suspiciously*) Are you sure we've not met?

Marjory Not to my knowledge.

Joan (*frowning*) I've always been good with faces. Not often I make a mistake. (*Proudly*) Should have been in the p'lice, according to my first husband. (*She slips her shoe back on*) So what brings you here? One of their "regulars", are you? Or just bad luck?

Marjory (*slightly taken aback*) I'd hardly call it bad luck, Mrs Reece. The owners are nice, the food is good, rooms clean and comfortable. And even you must agree the surroundings are impressive.

Joan (*scowling*) I'd take Barbados, any day. Or Venice. (*Bitterly*) I'd even settle for Leeds, Birmingham or Blackpool. Anywhere but this place. It's so flamin' dead, we might as well be on the moon.

Marjory (*mildly*) There's a lot to be said for peace and quiet in this day and age.

Joan Only by them who've never been young. I had all that crap from my first husband and I'll not make the same mistake twice. This time round it's bright lights and high livin'. Not Poverty Row.

Marjory (*gently*) Then why choose a country guest-house for Christmas? (*Apologetically*) I couldn't help overhearing.

Joan (*embarrassed*) Seemed a good idea at the time. I'd seen that film on telly. You know? *Gosford Park*. Load of posh buggers trying to out-do each other with their airs and graces. Quite fancied myself mingling with gentry like that lot. I could have put them straight on a thing or two, I can tell you. (*Seething*) But no. We had to come here. Stuck up the backside of England and not able to get a decent night's sleep for all the screeching and bloody moaning. First night we stayed here, I thought the place was haunted. (*Tartly*) Didn't bother him, of course. If I hadn't stuck my elbow in his ribs, he'd have slept right through it.

Marjory (*curiously*) And what was it? The thing that disturbed you?

Joan Flaming fox, according to the Lockwoods. But it sounded like someb'dy in agony, to me. And as for that bloody owl, if it starts hooting again tonight, I'm out of here first thing tomorrow.

Derek Tyndale appears in the doorway. He is a slender man in his early forties with an apologetic manner, wearing a padded car coat over a tweed suit with matching waistcoat, and clutching hat and gloves. He pauses to unzip the car coat

Derek (*shyly*) Afternoon, ladies. I *thought* I heard voices. (*To Marjory*) Did you find your way all right?

Marjory To the village, you mean? (*She shakes her head*) I thought discretion was the better part of valour. It's nothing urgent and I've all week to get myself organized.

Derek (*helpfully*) If you'd like a lift, you've only to say the word. It's no trouble. I pass through it every morning and there's a nice little tea-room on the High Street if you find yourself feeling peckish.

Joan (*with distaste*) Spare me from getting that desperate.
Derek (*frowning*) It's not bad, actually. Whenever we stayed here, Mother called in to soak up the atmosphere. Said it recharged her batteries.
Marjory (*reassuringly*) I know just what she means, Mr Tyndale. I'm the same with Fortnum and Mason. She's not with you this time?
Derek (*forcing a smile*) Not this time. She died two years ago.
Marjory (*quickly*) Oh, I am sorry.
Derek (*brightly*) But I still come down myself. Every so often. Just for a day or two. It may seem strange, but I feel close to her here. She was very fond of the old *Harlequin*.
Marjory (*interested*) So you knew it in the old days? Before the alterations?
Derek (*moving into the room*) Oh, yes. She even thought of buying it, once. (*Regretfully*) Didn't work out, though. But they're doing a great job. The Lockwoods. Better than I'd have done. (*Smiling*) Well — must pop upstairs and get my notes written up or the publishers'll be breathing down my neck and wanting their advance back. (*He turns to exit*)
Joan (*archly*) I didn't realize you were a writer, Mr Tyndale.
Derek (*awkwardly*) Only a minor one. It's not a family thing. Mum was the lady of letters. She had three books published before I was born.
Marjory (*enthused*) You must give me her name. Perhaps I've read her?
Derek (*slightly embarrassed*) I don't think they'll be your kind of thing, Mrs Pike. They're more of a — specialist nature.
Marjory (*amused*) Don't judge a book by its cover, Mr Tyndale. I like a good bodice ripper. Even at my age.
Derek (*hastily*) Oh, no. They're nothing like that. They're not fiction. They're about her work.
Joan And what was that?

Sally hurries in

Sally Sorry to break in, but there's a call for Mrs Pike. (*To her*) Chantelle Vincent?
Marjory (*frowning*) Who?
Sally It's rather urgent, she said. (*Helpfully*) You can take it at the end of the hall. Next to the first aid box. Bryan's putting it through for you.

Marjory puts down her postcards, still looking puzzled, and rises

Marjory I can't place the name at all. It doesn't ring bells. (*She hesitates*) And how did she know I was here? The only one I told was Aileen. (*Recovering*) Do excuse me.

Marjory exits

Sally (*moving to the rear windows*) Just got back in time, Derek. First flakes are falling. (*She closes the curtains on both the windows*)

Derek (*enthusiastically*) White Christmas coming up, eh?.

Sally (*amused*) So long as it's not *too* white. We were snowed in for days three years ago. (*She moves down to the window* L) And we had a power cut. Almost ended up eating each other. (*She closes the curtains*) But we're ready for it this time. All the old chimneys have been unblocked and there's enough wood out back to last us a month. If the worst comes to the worst, we'll not be cold or hungry. (*She moves back towards the door*) Anyone fancy a drink?

Joan I'll settle for a sherry if there's one on offer.

Derek Oh ... er ... coffee's fine for me.

Sally (*smiling*) One coffee and one sherry. (*To Joan*) Sweet, medium or dry?

Joan Drier the better.

Sally I'll be back in a second.

Sally exits

Derek (*after a slight pause*) Nice coat.

Joan (*glancing at him askance*) Know about furs, do you?

Derek (*embarrassed*) Not really. There was one in Mum's wardrobe when she died. Bit lighter than yours, I think. Hadn't worn it in years. Not since the fuss started, anyway. You know? Animal rights thing. Didn't do to upset the fans.

Joan (*scornfully*) Took notice of them, did she? Well more fool her. I'd like to see anybody tell me what I could or couldn't wear.

Derek (*uncomfortably*) It's always a problem when you're in the public eye. She was very — sensitive.

Joan (*tartly*) Bite before you're bitten's my motto. I may look soft, but I'm not just a pretty face. If folks come looking for trouble in my direction, they'll be in for a big surprise.

Derek (*jokingly*) Like the Teddy Bears' Picnic, eh?

Joan looks at him as though he's gone mad

Sally enters

Sally I'm sorry, Mrs Reece. We're totally out of dry sherry. Will medium be all right? I'll have more in, tomorrow.

Joan (*acidly*) If I'd wanted medium, I'd have said.

Sally (*hopefully*) I can offer a white wine.

Joan (*scowling*) Better than nothing, I suppose. But in my opin ... (*She stops in mid-sentence as the thought strikes her*) That's where I know her from. I knew I recognized her. (*Smugly*) The Pike woman. Her name's not Pike at all. She's here under false pretences.

Sally and Derek stare at Joan

> She's Caroline Faye.

Sally (*blankly*) Who?

Derek looks ashen

Joan (*smirking*) Caroline Faye. Had a column in one of the daily rags a few years back. Exposing con merchants and the like. You must have seen it. Old bitch wrote a book when they dropped her and caused a right stink in some quarters. (*Amused*) Closed half the Spiritualist Churches in England.

Sally (*wide-eyed*) Really?

Joan (*dismissively*) First husband bought me a copy, but I never got round to reading it. I'd more to do with me life than worry about fake mediums ripping the bloody public off.

Derek (*in stricken tones*) It was lies. All lies. Not a grain of truth in it.

Joan (*airily*) I wouldn't know. But it didn't stop it selling, did it? (*Sourly*) Couldn't read a paper for weeks without somebody going on about it. Must have made her a fortune. Nothing like a scandal to help the sales figures.

Sally Scandal?

Joan (*wrinkling her nose*) Some poor cow topped herself after madam spilled the beans. Overdosed on drain cleaner, or something. (*Amused*) Ten minutes after the news broke, the rest of 'em were digging their crystal balls out and trying to contact her. (*Scornfully*) Talk about pathetic.

Sally And you're sure it's her? This — Caroline Faye? You couldn't be mistaken?

Joan (*pityingly*) I don't do mistakes, Mrs Lockwood. She may be using a false name, but if she's not Caroline Faye, I'll eat my bloody handbag.

Derek (*faintly*) Excuse me. I don't feel well. (*He turns unsteadily to exit*)

Sally (*concerned*) Derek?

Derek (*distractedly*) I'd no idea. I didn't think. (*He tries to push past Sally*)

Sally (*alarmed*) Would you like me to call a doctor?

Derek (*wildly*) You don't understand. It was her. The one who killed my mother. (*Glaring at Joan; bitterly*) She was the "poor cow" who "topped herself".

Derek hurries out of the room

Joan's eyes widen

Sally (*hurrying after Derek; calling*) Derek. Mr Tyndale.

Sally exits

Joan (*rolling her eyes*) Whoopsy-daisy. (*She opens her handbag, takes out her compact and peers at herself in the mirror. She fishes out a lipstick and applies some, then inspects herself again*)

A moment later, Marjory enters

Marjory (*pleasantly*) Sorry about that. You never know *who* you're talking to these days, do you? (*Surprised*) Oh — has Mr Tyndale gone? (*She sits in the armchair*) I hope I missed nothing exciting? (*She picks up her postcards*) It's still snowing, by the way. If it carries on the way it is, we'll be having a most interesting Christmas.
Joan (*slowly*) Yes. (*To herself*) I rather think we might.

Marjory begins to write

CURTAIN

SCENE 2

An hour later

The tea things have been cleared but the room is otherwise unchanged

Sally sits on the settee looking worried. Bryan is perched on the arm beside her. He is wearing his chef's white tunic and trousers

Bryan I don't see what we can do about it. It's none of our business. We can't toss her out like an orphan from a workhouse.
Sally (*protesting*) But you should have seen the state of him.
Bryan I know. I know. You said. But who's to say he's not over-reacting?
Sally (*incredulously*) I'd hardly call it over-reacting when your mother commits suicide. (*Bitterly*) Of all the places in all the world ——
Bryan (*finishing the near-quote*) — why did she turn up here? (*He stands*) Well, like I said. We can hardly ask her to leave.
Sally (*firmly*) If she doesn't, he will. He said so.
Bryan (*glumly*) Looks like another empty room, then. Just what we need right now.
Sally So what do we do?
Bryan (*shrugging*) Get on with dinner as normal — and leave 'em to fight it out.
Sally (*protesting*) But what if Derek goes? He's one of our regulars.
Bryan We're running a guest house, love, not a Citizens' Advice. If he goes, he goes. It's up to him.

Sally (*suddenly*) I'll have a word with her. (*She stands*)

Bryan (*firmly*) Leave it alone. They can sort it themselves.

Sally (*insisting*) But she doesn't even realize. If she knew the situation, she'd probably be off like a shot.

Bryan Why's that? If what you're saying's true, she'll be convinced she's done the public a favour. They don't like being ripped off, love.

Sally But it was all a pack of lies. He said so.

Bryan Then why didn't he sue her? They sue at the drop of a hat, these days. And quite frankly, the idea of a few dozen Madame Arcatis getting their just deserts doesn't exactly upset me.

Sally (*acidly*) So you wouldn't mind if they all took an overdose of drain cleaner?

Bryan Not particularly. If the local bank manager was helping himself to the cash in your savings account, you'd be only too pleased if somebody blew the whistle on him. Right? And if he chose to top himself rather than face the music, then that's his choice. You can't do the time, you don't do the crime.

Sally (*after a moment*) You really don't see it, do you? You haven't a clue. (*She turns from him and moves* DL)

Bryan (*blankly*) About what?

Sally (*turning to face him*) They've been coming here for years. Derek helped you re-roof the shed.

Bryan (*protesting*) I didn't ask him. He volunteered.

Sally (*hotly*) Of course he volunteered. He's that kind of person. He wouldn't have taken payment if you'd offered it.

Bryan I did.

Sally (*curbing her temper*) What I'm trying to say is they were nice people. I liked Mrs Tyndale, no matter what Caroline Faye thought. (*Stricken*) I'd no idea she'd killed herself. He never even hinted at it.

Bryan You can hardly blame him. But I don't see why you're working yourself up about it. She was pleasant enough, but she was only a customer. And from all accounts, a teensy bit of a con merchant.

Sally From Caroline Faye's account, you mean. (*Firmly*) Well she may think she's somebody special, but I don't want her in this house, thank you very much. (*She moves behind the settee, heading for the door*)

Bryan (*moving to intercept her*) And how are you thinking of getting her out? Unless you've a good excuse, there's not a cat in hell's chance.

Sally We could tell her we know who she really is. That she's here under false pretences.

Bryan And how would that help? Using a false name's not exactly unknown in the hospitality trade. And what if is her real name? The other one could be a *nom de plume*, or whatever they call it. Doris Day was Doris Kappelhoff.

Sally I don't care about Doris Day. I just want that woman out of here.

Bryan (*lightly*) Would you like me to bash her over the head with the steak hammer? I could chop her up later and pop her out with the kitchen waste.

Sally (*balefully*) I sometimes wonder about your sanity.

Bryan (*wearily*) Sal.

Sally I'll sort something out myself.

Sally brushes past him and exits

Bryan heaves a deep sigh

Lionel (*off; calling*) Mrs Lockwood? Mrs Lockw ... (*Disgustedly*) And up yours, *too*, dear.

Bryan (*moving into the doorway and speaking into the hall*) Was there something you wanted, Mr ... (*he fumbles to remember the name*) Reece?

Lionel (*off*) Sorry. Didn't see you in there. Any chance of a pre-dinner snifter or two?

Bryan (*forcing a smile*) I think we can manage that. (*He steps back*) Wine or sherry?

Lionel enters. He is a disagreeable man in his fifties, though possessing charisma when he chooses to display it. He wears expensive casual clothes, and showy jewellery

Lionel Glass of red'll do. Can't stand the other muck. (*He glances round*) First one down, am I?

Bryan (*smiling tightly*) Still half an hour. Rest'll be down soon, I expect.

Lionel Including the resident poisoner? (*He moves to the settee*)

Bryan (*puzzled*) Sorry?

Lionel (*sitting*) Mrs Whatsername? The new arrival.

Bryan (*uneasily*) I'd be careful what I said, if I were you. She could have you up for slander.

Lionel (*grinning*) Not if I claimed "fair comment". Half the nutters in England'd back me up. (*Easily*) But you needn't worry. I'll mind my p's and q's. Though I can't say the same for Joanie. Got a mouth on her like a basking shark, that one.

Bryan (*stiffly*) I'll get you that drink.

Bryan exits

Lionel (*leaning back and singing quietly*) Bring me flesh and bring me wine, I'm not melancholy. Just an hour or two to go and I'll be in the lo-lly ...

There is the sound of a small bell. Lionel looks towards the hall. The bell sounds again. There are a few moments of silence

Isobel (*off*) Hallo? Anybody there?

Lionel rises, moves to the doorway and looks out

(*Off*) Hallo?

The bell sounds again

(*Off; startled*) Oh. (*She gives an embarrassed laugh*) You gave me a start. I thought ... (*Beginning again*) Mr Lockwood?
Lionel (*putting on the charm*) 'Fraid not, m'dear. Just one of the humble guests. He'll be back in a second, though. You can wait in here if you like. It's a bit more hospitable. (*He steps back*)
Isobel (*off; doubtfully*) You're sure it's all right?
Lionel So long as you don't drip on the Wilton. You can hang your coat on the stand, there. (*He moves* DL *of the sofa again*)
Isobel (*off*) I'd better leave my shoes, too. They're a bit of a mess.
Lionel (*calling*) Come far, have you? Bloody awful night for it.

Isobel Clarke enters hesitantly. She is a striking young woman in her late twenties, dressed in jeans and polo-neck sweater

Isobel Just down the road, actually. Paying a surprise visit to friends who surprised me by not even being there. Neighbour said they left for Bermuda last Wednesday. (*Enviously*) Lucky devils.
Lionel (*sitting*) Been there yourself, have you?
Isobel (*scoffing*) Chance'd be a fine thing. Not on my salary.
Lionel (*indicating for Isobel to sit*) Shouldn't shed too many tears. Not half as exotic as it sounds. Place we stayed in had cockroaches the size of Alsatians. Only thing that scared 'em was the wife. (*He chortles*) Lionel Reece, by the way.
Isobel (*smiling*) Isobel Clarke.
Lionel So what brings you to this place?
Isobel (*wryly*) I lost an argument with a four-by-four. Ended up in a ditch about a mile from here. (*She sits in the armchair*)
Lionel (*feigning concern*) All right, are you? Not hurt?
Isobel (*lightly*) A bit shaken up when it happened, but the car got the worst of it. I swerved to avoid him on a blind bend and lost control. By the time I stopped shaking and climbed out, he'd vanished down the hill.
Lionel (*tightly*) Bastard.

Isobel (*shaking her head*) He wouldn't have seen a thing the way the snow was falling, and in any case, it was my fault. I was well over his side of the road. (*Ruefully*) The worst thing was, I couldn't get through to anybody for help. My mobile was dead and I hadn't even a torch with me. If I hadn't seen this place when I went by earlier, I'd have spent the night on the back seat with a blanket wrapped round me.

Lionel (*giving a shark-like smile*) Well, thank God it didn't come to that. You could have frozen to death. Is ... Er ... Is there anyone at home you need to get in touch with? It's a bit of a dead spot for mobiles in this part — we found that out yesterday — but there's a land-line down the hall.

Isobel (*shaking her head*) I was going to call my breakdown service, but I wouldn't fancy the chances of getting them out here tonight. Not the way it is. I'll just book a room and sort it out in the morning.

Bryan enters with a glass of red wine

Lionel (*spotting Bryan*) Ah. Mine host, himself.

Isobel (*rising*) Mr Lockwood? (*She smiles*) Isobel Clarke. (*Extending her hand*) Sorry to land myself on you like this, but I've had an accident up the road and appear to be stranded. Please tell me you're not fully booked for tonight.

Bryan (*shaking Isobel's hand, slightly flustered*) No. No. Of course not. You can have the *Harlequin* room. It's a double, actually, but we can do it as a single under the circumstances. (*Concerned*) An accident, you said? Is anyone hurt?

Isobel (*quickly*) No, no. Just my pride.

Bryan (*relieved*) I'll get Sally to book you in, then. (*He hands the glass to Lionel, begins to retreat then pauses*) Will you want to eat with us? We're doing dinner in fifteen minutes or so.

Isobel (*gratefully*) I wouldn't say no. I've only had coffee since breakfast.

Bryan (*nodding*) Right. She ... Er ... She'll be with you in a minute, then.

Bryan exits

Isobel (*approvingly*) Nice man.

Lionel (*sneering*) Bit of a wimp, if you ask me. (*He sips at his wine. Grudgingly*) But he's not a bad cook. Wasting his time here, though. He'd be better off running some fancy restaurant in Manchester and making real money.

Isobel (*sitting again*) P'raps he prefers country life? I wouldn't mind a crack at it myself. Especially in this area.

Lionel (*sourly*) It'd drive me round the bend. City man, myself. Like a fish out of water when I'm out of the bright lights.

Isobel (*amused*) So what are you doing in Derbyshire?

Lionel Not my idea, believe me. Wife fancied Christmas in a country house so I booked us in. Total waste of time. (*He grimaces*) She's done nothing but bitch about it since we got here. (*He gulps at his drink*)

Isobel (*sympathetically*) Not really what she expected, eh?

Lionel (*sourly*) It never is. If life were bloody Harrods, she'd spend it in the complaints department. Wouldn't think she were nowt but a shop assistant when I met her. They were glad to see the back of her at Superdrug, believe you me.

Marjory pokes her head round the door and sees them. Smiling, she enters. She wears a top-coat and carries a small umbrella, a few postcards and a long envelope

Marjory (*apologetically*) Sorry to interrupt, but there's no-one in the dining-room and I'm popping down to the post-box. (*She shows them the letters*) They'll go first thing, so I'm told, and I'd like them to arrive before Christmas. It's always difficult, this time of year, what with greetings cards as well. I shouldn't be long, but if anyone *does* ask ... (*She smiles and turns to exit again*)

Isobel (*rising*) Would you like me to take them? It's a bit slippery underfoot and my jacket's wet already.

Marjory (*turning back*) That's very kind, but I wouldn't dream of imposing. It's only a few yards and the air will do me good. (*Confidentially*) The heating's a bit too efficient in my room, I'm afraid. (*After a hesitation*) I wonder if they'd lower it if I asked? Even *Columbine* looks flushed.

Isobel (*blankly*) Columbine?

Marjory The painting. Over the fireplace. Such a charming idea and so well done. I must see the rest before I go.

Lionel (*sourly*) You could take the one in our room. Looks like a bloody ghoul with all that white stuff plastered over his face. And as for his eyes ... They're enough to give you the willies.

Marjory (*smiling*) You'll be in *Clown*, then? (*To Isobel*) And *Pantaloon* or *Harlequin*, I expect? (*Explaining*) Miss Seton's in *Scaramouche*. Next door to me.

Isobel (*at a loss*) I've not booked in yet, but — yes. Mr Lockwood did say something about *Harlequin*, though I wasn't sure ... I mean ... They use names here instead of room numbers?

Marjory (*nodding*) In memory of Jeremiah Jenkins. A famous Harlequin in Victorian times. (*Ruefully*) Though I can't say there'll be many who'll know his name today. (*Brightly*) But he lived here after his accident. Pamela will tell you about it if you're interested — and the bonus, of course, is he actually died in your room. (*She beams at Isobel*)

Isobel (*not too thrilled at the news*) Really?

Marjory (*realizing*) Oh, my goodness. I can't believe I said that. (*Flustered*) I'm so sorry. Aileen's always telling me to put brain in gear before speaking. I do tend to blurt things out and it gets me into so much trouble.

Lionel (*drily*) So we'd heard.

Marjory (*looking at him, puzzled*) I'm sorry?

Lionel (*easily*) Speaking out of turn. The wrong word in the wrong place and you find yourself with all sorts of problems. (*He smiles falsely*) Look at newspaper wallahs, for instance. They'll write any old crap to keep their names in print, but do they ever think what happens to the folk who read it? (*He shakes his head*) Remember Caroline Faye?

Isobel (*blankly*) Who?

Lionel (*to Isobel*) Caroline Faye. Had a gossip column in one of the dailies just a few years back. Right old bitch, she was. Got herself sacked for upsetting too many readers. One of 'em even killed herself. (*Thoughtfully*) I wonder what happened to her? Changed her name, I expect. (*To Marjory*) What do you think, darlin'?

Marjory (*looking at Lionel strangely*) I've no idea. I've never heard of her.

Lionel (*smiling*) Not interested in spirits, then? Ghosts and ghoulies and things that go bump in the night?

Marjory (*uncertainly*) Only if Dickens wrote about them.

Lionel (*easily*) You'd have liked old Caroline, then. Not too keen herself on things ethereal. Wouldn't mind meeting her, some day. Providing she's still alive. (*He beams falsely*) We could talk about con merchants and such.

Isobel (*amused*) Do you know any con merchants?

Lionel In my line of business? (*He chuckles*) You can't walk for tripping on 'em. (*Easily*) I might write a book one day and expose the lot. (*He glances at Marjory for her reaction*)

Isobel (*lightly*) And what is your line of business, Mr Reece? If you don't mind my asking.

Lionel (*smugly*) Let's just say it's "keeping an eye on things and looking after the cash flow".

Isobel (*archly*) Mmm. Very mysterious.

Marjory (*at a loss*) Well ... I'd better be off or I'll never get these in the post. (*To Isobel*) And do accept my apologies. I didn't mean to upset you. It happened a very long time ago.

Isobel (*reassuringly*) It's all right. As long as I don't have to share with his ghost, I'll be fine. (*She smiles*)

Marjory smiles back and exits

Lionel (*to Isobel*) Believe in that stuff, do you? Reincarnation, et cetera?

Isobel (*shaking her head*) But I try to keep an open mind. (*She sits again*) This woman you mentioned — Caroline Faye. Now I think about it, the name does sound vaguely familiar.

Lionel Be surprised if it didn't. Case went on for weeks before they threw it out. Left the court without a stain on her character. (*Snorting*) British justice. I'd have thrown the bloody *book* at her.

Isobel (*frowning*) Remind me.

Lionel Got herself sued for libel and God knows what else. But she obviously knew where the bodies were buried and wriggled off the hook. Only good thing that came of it was she upped sticks and vanished. Popular thought was she'd taken her poison pen to warmer climes — South Africa or New Zealand—but nobody knew for certain. Last place you'd expect her to turn up is here. (*He gulps at his wine*)

Isobel (*surprised*) Here?

Sally hurries into the room

Sally (*apologetically*) Mrs Clarke?

Isobel rises

Isobel Miss, actually.

Sally (*extending her hand*) Sally Lockwood.

They touch fingers

Sorry to have kept you waiting. I was down in the wine cellar. I'll book you in now, shall I? It won't take a minute, then I'll show you the room before dinner. (*She heads for the door again*)

Isobel follows her

The bedding's goose-down, but if you're allergic to feathers, we've plenty of sheets and blankets. And if you've any dietary problems, you've only to mention it and we'll do our best to sort something out ...

Isobel and Sally exit into the hall

We already do vegetarian and gluten free and the rest's totally organic.

Lionel settles back on the settee and gulps at his wine contentedly. There is a short silence

Joan hurriedly limps in

Joan (*scornfully*) I might have known you'd be chucking that stuff down your throat. Can't even wait for dinner. (*She glances behind her then moves closer to him*) Well, you needn't bother settling yourself in. We can eat on the way back.

Lionel Eh? (*He sits up*)

Joan (*balefully*) You heard. We're leaving. I've packed the bags already. They can keep their over-priced doss-house — and stuff bloody Derbyshire where the sun don't shine. I'm not spending my Christmas in this place and that's final.

Lionel (*glowering*) So where do you suggest we go?

Joan (*hissing*) I don't bloody care. Anywhere'll do as long as it's not here.

Lionel (*realizing*) So who's bitten your bum this time?

Joan (*sharply*) I beg your pardon?

Lionel Who's upset you?

Joan (*bridling*) I don't know what you mean.

Lionel (*coldly*) Since we got here yesterday, you've done nothing but bitch and moan about everybody and everything. Then a couple of hours ago, you recognize Caroline Faye and everything changes. You can't stop talking about her and what's going on down here. There's a nice juicy scandal on the cards and you're frantic for a ringside seat with all the bloody trimmings. Now suddenly — suddenly — it's all changed and you're wanting to leave. So I'm asking again. Who's bitten your fat, flabby bum?

Joan (*loath to admit it*) I made a mistake. It's not her.

Lionel What isn't?

Joan (*tightly*) The Pike woman. She's not Caroline Faye. (*She turns away from him*)

Lionel (*puzzled*) But you recognized her. You said so.

Joan (*seething*) I thought I recognized her. She must be her bloody twin.

Lionel Then what made you change your mind?

Joan (*grudgingly*) I rang Melissa. From upstairs. (*She turns back to him*) You can get a signal if you open the window and lean out a bit.

Lionel (*heavily*) And?

Joan She told me. It was in the *Mirror* last year. Caroline Faye died of cancer. In Portugal.

Lionel (*after a slight pause*) So who is the Pike woman?

Joan (*bitterly*) How should I know? Exactly who she says she is.

Lionel (*amused*) So that's why you want to get away? You've put your pretty size sevens right in the middle of the poo-poo?

Joan (*tightly*) I'm not telling that lot I made a mistake. If we leave now, we'll be well away before they find out. We can find somewhere else, easily.

(*Smugly*) There's no shortage of room when you've got the cash — even at Christmastime.

Lionel (*raising an eyebrow*) Oh? You've come into money, have you?

Joan frowns

(*Harshly*) Forgive me for being on the thick side — but I was under the impression that what I had in my bank account happened to be mine.

Joan (*uncertainly*) Well — of course it's yours.

Lionel I supply the cash, and you provide eye-candy, if and when the need arises.

Joan (*huffily*) I wouldn't exactly phrase it in those terms.

Lionel (*flatly*) No. I'm damn sure you wouldn't.

Joan (*stung*) We happen to be married.

Lionel (*rising*) That's right. We do. (*With menace*) And if you'd like us to stay that way, you'll keep your big mouth shut for the next few days and pretend to enjoy yourself.

Joan (*staring at him in disbelief*) You can't talk to me like that.

Lionel (*advancing on her*) In case you'd forgotten, sweetheart, you need me a damn sight more than I need you. If it wasn't for me, you'd still be dishing out corn-plasters, and buying your frocks in Oxfam. We came down here because I had a job to do. And like it or not, we're going nowhere till it's over and done with. (*He pushes his empty glass into her hand*) Now get upstairs and start unpacking. I'll see you in the dining-room.

Lionel exits

Joan stands open-mouthed, then, seething with rage, rushes to the door to scream abuse at Lionel. Before she can speak, however, she stops dead in the doorway, a look of surprise on her face. Hastily recoiling, she attempts to hide herself from view by flattening herself against the bookcase

Sally (*off; surprised*) Derek. (*Concerned*) Oh, my God.

Derek (*off*) It's all right. There's nothing broken. I slipped on one of the stepping stones.

Sally (*off; concerned*) You're bleeding.

Derek (*off*) Only a graze. (*Laughing unsteadily*) Worse things happen at sea.

Sally (*off*) Let me get the first aid. I'll find you a plaster. Go through to the lounge.

Joan looks around frantically

Derek (*off*) You don't have to bother ...

Sally (*off; firmly*) Lounge.

Derek enters the lounge. He wears his quilted car-coat which is now glistening with melted snow, as is his hair, and he holds his injured right hand which is heavily blood-smeared. A series of scratch marks begin below his right eye and extend across his cheek; these are also bleeding. Without noticing Joan, he limps his way behind the settee to the armchair L

Joan furtively slips from her position of concealment and exits

Derek stands by the chair, his eyes closed and a slight smile on his lips

A moment later, Pamela enters. She is dressed for dinner in a smart skirt, cream shirt and a cardigan

Pamela (*seeing him*) Derek?

Derek opens his eyes and turns to face Pamela

(*Noticing his injuries*) Oh my God.
Derek (*lightly*) Exactly what Sally said.
Pamela (*concerned*) What happened? (*She moves towards Derek*)
Derek (*shakily*) I fell in the stream and knocked myself silly. You'd think I'd know better by now. I've been coming here long enough.
Pamela (*briskly*) Let's get your coat off. I can't look you over when you're wrapped up like a mummy. (*She fumbles with his coat buttons*)
Derek (*amused*) I didn't know you were *a doctor*.
Pamela When you're English and Drama at North Lane, you do everything from finger paints to brain surgery. But just to put your mind at rest, I'm also in the St John's. (*Frowning*) What on earth were you doing outside in this lot? (*She helps him off with the coat*) Sit down.

Derek sits in the armchair; Pamela puts his coat on the settee

You're sure nothing's *broken?* (*She takes his hand*)
Derek (*wincing*) Oww ...
Pamela Sorry. Wriggle your fingers.

Derek patiently does so

(*Sighing*) Well, they're all in working order. And the bleeding's stopped. (*She tilts his face to look at the scratches*) But I don't like the look of your face.

Derek Thank you.

Pamela (*giving a mock glower*) You know what I mean. (*She releases him*) The sooner we get those cleaned up, the better.

Sally hurries in with a small tray on which rests a box of plasters, a small bowl of water and a roll of cotton wool

Sally Here we are. Flying nurse to the rescue. (*She moves between Pamela and Derek, sinks to her knees and puts the tray on the floor*)

Pamela I've checked him for breaks, but he seems to be clear.

Sally (*tearing cotton wool*) Thank goodness for that. The last thing we need is a trip to the Health Centre at this time of night. Assuming of course there's anybody there. (*She dips the cotton wool in the water and dabs gently at the palm of Derek's hand*) Does that hurt?

Derek (*unconcerned*) It's only a graze. I told you.

Sally (*still dabbing*) Looks like you've had it in the veg slicer. (*Sighing*) Oh, Derek. You're going to need a bandage for this and there's none in the box.

Pamela There's a couple of crêpe ones in my room. In case of a twisted ankle.

Sally (*relieved*) Would you mind, Pammy?

Pamela heads for the door

And could you check the box for antiseptic cream? I think there's a tube of Savlon.

Pamela exits

(*To Derek*) You're going to need something on it. (*Concerned*) What on earth were you doing?

Derek (*embarrassed*) Making a fool of myself, I expect. I shouldn't have made such a fuss this afternoon. You know ...

Sally (*still cleaning the wound*) You'd every right, Derek. It was our fault. If we'd known what had happened, we wouldn't have let her near the place. We're so sorry.

Derek (*protesting*) No, no, it was my fault for not saying anything. You couldn't have known. (*After a hesitation*) Tyndale's our real name, you see, but she worked as Dorothy Tinker. That's what they called her at the Inquest and that's who the public thought she was. (*Dreamily*) Mrs Dorothy Tinker. Clairvoyant. (*Earnestly*) They still send her letters, you know.

Sally (*pre-occupied*) Really?

Derek (*explaining*) They don't believe it, you see? The things that were said about her. They know she wasn't a fake. She really could reach the other side. She'd proved it. Time after time after time. (*Suddenly distracted*) But she worried. That the ones she'd been helping might think that she'd fleeced them and hate her for it. (*Hastily*) I told her she was wrong, of course, but she wouldn't listen. Just sat in her chair for hours on end with tears streaming down her cheeks and a terrible blank look on her face. (*Quietly*) Then two days later she killed herself ...

Sally (*sympathetically*) It must have been awful for you.

Derek (*nodding*) I didn't know what to do at first. She'd always been there, you see. And suddenly she'd gone. I was on my own for the first time in my life. (*Embarrassed*) Not very masculine, I suppose, but I had a kind of breakdown. Even considered my own suicide. At least we'd be together again. (*Suddenly smiling*) But then it happened. She came back to me.

Sally (*blankly*) Back? (*She looks up at him*)

Derek (*brightly*) "Don't you worry," she said. "I may be gone in the flesh, but I'll always be *with* you." And she has been. (*Beaming*) She's stayed with me ever since. Telling me what to do and how to manage. We communicate, you see.

Sally (*uneasily*) I see ...

Derek It was the shock of meeting her — the Faye woman — that upset me. It was so unexpected, I had to get away. I've been wandering round the hills since I left here. Trying to get my head straight. And that's where Mum found me again. "Now calm down, Derek," she said. "You're making things very difficult for people who don't deserve it. They're our friends. You can't take it out on them. Leaving them with an empty room just isn't on." And she was right, of course. You are our friends. "But what about her?" I said. "That vicious and spiteful woman?" "You mustn't let her upset you," she said. "I've got lots of friends on this side, and they'll deal with Caroline Faye for us." (*He beams at her*) So I took her advice and came back.

Sally (*at a loss*) That's — lovely.

Derek I'm not late for dinner, am I?

Sally (*quickly*) No. No. Of course not. I — er — I'll just finish cleaning you up and then we'll start serving. You can have yours in your room, if you'd like?

Derek It's all right. I'll eat in the dining-room. (*Beaming*) She won't upset me now. She'll never upset me again. Just give me a minute to change and I'll be right down. (*Grimacing*) I'm a bit damp round the nether regions.

Pamela enters with a crêpe bandage and a tube of ointment

Pamela These should do the trick. (*She moves to Sally and Derek*) Would you like me to swathe him while you keep an eye on the kitchen? Bryan's just rushed upstairs to change his top. Looks like he's had an argument with the gravy and lost. Your attendance might be appreciated.

Sally (*rising, relieved*) If you wouldn't mind. (*Awkwardly*) I ... er ... I'll tidy up while everyone's eating.

Sally hurries from the room

Derek (*plaintively*) I'm not helpless, you know. I can do a bandage as well as the next man.

Pamela (*unimpressed*) Now where've I heard that before? Stick your hand out and keep quiet whilst I anoint the soothing balm. (*She tucks the bandage under her arm and unscrews the top of the ointment*)

Derek (*apprehensively*) Do you think it'll sting?

Pamela I sincerely *hope so. I* love seeing strong men weep. Hand.

Derek reluctantly extends his hand and Pamela squeezes the ointment on to it. Re-capping the tube, she stoops and drops it on to the tray, picking up a pad of cotton wool before straightening. She presses the pad gently on to the ointment, then extracts the bandage and begins to wrap Derek's hand

We'll look at it again tomorrow. If it's turned green during the night, I'll amputate first thing. Don't want to take risks, do we? In the meantime, I'd leave the knife alone and try eating with your fork.

Derek Are you always this sadistic?

Pamela Oh, yes. Comes from bottling up my frustrations with brain-dead governors, incompetent Ofsted inspectors, and a Head of Education who couldn't find her way out of a paper bag if they gave her a pair of scissors. (*She finishes wrapping his hand*) There.

Derek (*inspecting it*) Thank you.

Pamela Now for your face. (*She stoops to the tray again and picks up a pad of cotton wool*) Looks like you've had a fight with a Bengal tiger. (*She damps the pad in the water*)

Derek (*absently covering the scratches with his bandaged hand*) I can do that myself.

Pamela (*shrugging*) Your choice. But it's not a pretty sight. You might need stitches in *one* of them.

Derek (*standing*) Probably looks worse than it is. But thanks for this, anyway. (*He shows his bandaged hand*) I'd better go up and change now. Mustn't be late for dinner. Won't do to upset the chef, will it? (*He gives a smile*)

Derek quickly exits

Pamela watches him go, then shakes her head and picks up the tray, dropping the wet pad on to it

Sally enters, looking harassed

Sally You've not seen Mrs Pike, have you? I can't find her anywhere and there's someone on the phone for her.
Pamela (*blankly*) Haven't a clue.
Sally (*frustrated*) Blasted woman. She's been nothing but trouble since she came here.
Pamela (*surprised*) We talking about the same person?
Sally (*dismissively*) I'll tell you about it later. They'll have to call back. (*She turns to leave*)
Pamela (*displaying the tray*) What shall I do with these?
Sally Just—leave them. (*She moves to the doorway, then hesitates*) Pammy?
Pamela Yes?
Sally (*doubtfully*) Do you think he's all right? Derek, I mean. He seems a bit ... (*She does not know what to say*)
Pamela Out of it? Yes. I thought so myself, at first, but he's fine now. I shouldn't worry yourself.
Sally (*unhappily*) But some of the *things* he said — it was almost as if——
Isobel (*off*) Mrs Lockwood?

Isobel enters, now wearing her shoes

You're looking for Mrs Pike, I hear? Is that the lady in *Columbine*?
Sally (*hopefully*) You haven't seen her, have you? There's a phone call ...
Isobel She was here a few minutes ago. She went to post some cards. I offered to do it for her, but she said she needed the air. (*Frowning*) Is she not back yet?
Pamela (*putting the tray on the table behind the settee*) Apparently not. (*To Sally*) Do you want me to check on her? See she's all right?
Sally (*shaking her head*) The devil takes care of his own. She'll just have to take her chances.

Sally exits

Isobel (*to Pamela, puzzled*) What was all that about?
Pamela I'm as much in the dark as you are. (*Lowering her voice and hissing*) But never mind her. What the hell are you doing here? I thought we'd agreed.
Isobel (*hissing*) I know. I know. But I didn't have much choice. The car's in a ditch about a mile away and I couldn't get hold of you. It was here or nowhere.
Pamela (*seething*) Then you should have stayed right where you *were*.
Isobel And frozen to death while I was at it? (*Sarcastically*) Oh, yes. And a fat lot of good that would have done. (*She moves* DR) Well don't get your

knickers in a twist. I'll be out of here first thing and you can carry on with
your goody-goody act as normal. All right?

Pamela *(following her down)* No, it's *not* all right. Have you *seen* it out
there? It's inches deep already and if it carries on, there'll be more than a
foot in the morning.

Isobel *(uninterested)* So?

Pamela *(coldly)* Do blocked roads and snow ploughs ring any bells?

Isobel *(snapping)* They'll hardly worry you. Up to your eyes in central
heating and general *bonhomie*. *(She turns away from Pamela)*

Pamela *(heavily)* It's not me I'm worried about.

Isobel *(acidly)* That's a pleasant change.

Pamela If everywhere's covered in snow ...

Sally enters

Sally I don't believe it. She's holding on. Must have money to burn.
(Hopefully) She's not back, I suppose?

Pamela *(turning to Sally)* Hasn't come in this way.

Sally *(tiredly)* You'd better go through. He's serving the soup now. No point
in everybody waiting.

Pamela *(frowning)* It's pretty bad out there. Are you sure you don't want me
to ——

Sally *(hastily)* No, no. Of course not. I mean — how long does it take to walk
to the post box and back? It's barely a hundred yards.

Isobel *(doubtfully)* She could have missed her footing. It wouldn't be
difficult on that path. I'd one or two stumbles myself.

Sally *(deciding)* I'd better stick my head out, then. *(She turns to leave)*

Pamela You wouldn't see past the bend. Go help Bryan. I'll see if she's on
her way.

Isobel *(hastily)* It's all right, Pammy. I'm not a soup person. I'll do it. You
get yours and I'll be back in a tick. My coat's still in the hall.

Sally *(to Isobel)* I hate imposing ...

Isobel *(smiling)* It's the least I can do for taking me in.

Isobel exits

Sally Nice woman.

Pamela *(coldly)* Seems to be. Yes. *(Diffidently)* I — er — don't suppose
you've seen the forecast?

Sally *(tiredly)* More of the same, by the sound of it. Thank God we're well
stocked. But it's a pity the Tysons cancelled. They'd have loved this lot.
White Christmas in Little Old England.

Pamela *(frowning)* That reminds me. I knew there was something I meant
to mention. Didn't you say Mr Tyson had left his pills behind?

Sally That's right.

Pamela And you'd put them in your first aid box?

Sally Yes.

Pamela (*making a moue*) Well, they're not there now. I noticed when I was looking for the Savlon.

Sally (*frowning*) They were there five minutes ago. I had them in my hand when I got the plasters. Are you sure you didn't miss them?

Pamela (*shrugging*) The only bottle I saw had oil of cloves in it.

Sally (*puzzled*) Maybe I put them down somewhere? I'll check when I put the other stuff back. (*Brightly*) It's not important, anyhow. It's not as if they're cyanide. (*Firmly*) Now scoot. If you keep his lordship's soup waiting, there'll be hell to pay. And you won't get the parson's nose at Christmas.

Isobel (*off; frantically*) Mrs Lockwood. Mrs Lockwood. Help.

Sally and Pamela turn as Isobel stumbles into the room. She is covered in snowflakes, but the front of her light-coloured jacket is bright red with blood

(*Gasping*) It's Mrs Pike. Someone's attacked her. Down by the wall. There's blood all over. (*She stares at her hands in horror*)

Pamela (*shocked*) How *is* she?

Isobel (*dazedly*) I think she's dead. (*Her eyes roll and she collapses to the floor in a faint*)

Sally and Pamela look at each other

CURTAIN

ACT II
SCENE 1

The same. Three hours later

Apart from the removal of the first aid things and a general tidy-up, the room is unchanged

Pamela is on the settee, lost in thought, the television remote control stick in her hand. Dialogue and bursts of laughter can be heard from the set. Derek, in clean casuals, sits at the table UL, doing a jigsaw puzzle, a gauze pad strapped to his cheek and his hand still bandaged. Lionel is sitting in the armchair DL, clutching a glass of red wine

There is a moment's pause

Lionel (*scornfully*) Don't know how you can watch that. Thirty years old if it's a day. Most of the buggers are dead.

There is no reaction

Bloody outrageous, I call it. Having to buy a licence when all you get for it's clapped out repeats and Big sodding Brother. (*He sips his drink*)
Derek (*mildly*) Would you please mind not doing that?
Lionel What? (*He glances round at Derek*)
Derek Using profanities. I think we can live without them. (*He puts a jigsaw piece in place*)
Lionel (*rudely*) You a *vicar*, or somethin'?
Derek No. But there's no need for foul language — especially in mixed company. (*He returns to his puzzle*)
Lionel (*amused*) She'll have heard worse where she comes from. (*To Pamela*) North Lane Community, isn't it?
Pamela (*snapping back to reality*) Hmm? (*She looks at Lionel*)
Lionel (*sneering*) Right bunch of toe-rags. Not a brain between 'em — or a civil tongue in their heads.
Pamela (*frowning*) Who hasn't?
Lionel Your lot. (*Sneering*) North Lane Community.
Pamela Oh. (*She clicks the television off*) An ex-pupil, are you?
Lionel (*frowning*) Eh?

Pamela I thought I recognized the manners. (*She puts the remote on the settee arm,* R)

Lionel (*harshly*) You don't need manners when you've plenty of brass. (*Smugly*) And believe me, lady, *I'm* not short of a bob or two. (*He drinks*)

Pamela (*drily*) So you keep reminding us. (*Sweetly*) And speaking of brass — we've not seen Mrs Reece lately. Having an early night, is she?

Lionel (*unsure of the insult*) She's not feeling too good. (*Recovering*) Hardly surprising when something like this happens. We came here for relaxation, not bumping into coppers whichever way we turned. If we'd wanted a murder weekend, we'd have bloody well booked one.

Pamela (*raising an eyebrow*) And who's been murdered? Or have I missed something? From what I understood, she missed her footing, hit her head on the wall and fractured her skull.

Lionel (*correcting her*) Appears to have missed her footing. Appears. They don't know for certain. (*He drinks*)

Pamela (*scornfully*) Of course they know. It's the only thing that could have happened. Look at Derek.

Derek looks up from the jigsaw

He almost ended up in the same boat. It's like an ice rink out there.

Derek returns to the puzzle

(*Pointedly*) And aren't you forgetting the footprints?

Lionel (*frowning*) What footprints?

Pamela The ones that should have been there if she had been attacked, but were rather conspicuously missing. When the police arrived, there was nothing but undisturbed snow from the road to the spot where we found her. Ergo — there was no attacker. It was an accident, pure and simple.

Lionel (*shrugging*) It's a good enough theory. And I'm sure the boys in blue'll be happy subscribing to it. (*Smugly*) But if anybody asked my opinion, I could give 'em another one that might be worth thinking about.

Pamela (*coldly*) Oh?

Lionel (*pointedly*) What if somebody from this place bashed her head in?

Derek looks up

Pamela (*after a moment, scornfully*) Don't be ridiculous. Why would anyone here want to kill her? She only arrived last night.

Lionel (*smirking*) Maybe she did — but I could still provide 'em with a damned good motive. (*He drinks*)

Pamela (*acidly*) I'd be most interested to hear it.

Lionel All right, then. Then how about this? Supposing a certain somebody found out she was here under false pretences? That she wasn't the harmless old biddy everybody thought she was? (*Lightly*) Now as far as I were concerned, she could have been Mother Teresa or Vera bloody Duckworth. It wouldn't have mattered a damn. But to someone with closer connections, she might have come across like the devil incarnate. Take him, for instance. (*He indicates Derek with his head*)

Pamela (*glancing at Derek in a puzzled manner*) What's he to do with it?

Lionel According to Joanie, he rushed out of here this afternoon thinking the old girl drove his mother to suicide. (*Triumphantly*) And if that's not a motive for bumping her off, I don't know what is. (*He smirks*)

Pamela (*looking at Derek in astonishment*) Derek? Is this true? Did you know Mrs Pike?

Derek (*defensively*) Not till I met her here. I'd never seen her before.

Pamela looks accusingly back at Lionel

(*Glowering*) But I knew what she'd done — and if Mrs Reece hadn't recognized her, there might never have been a chance to punish her.

Pamela (*turning back to him in astonishment*) Punish her?

Derek (*reasonably*) For killing Mother.

Lionel (*startled*) Hang on a minute. (*Rising*) You're not telling us you did kill her?

Derek (*disgustedly*) Of course I didn't.

Pamela (*relieved*) Thank God for that.

Derek (*coldly*) I'm not a fool. If I had killed her, they'd have sent me to gaol for years. They'd never have agreed that people like her deserved to die.

Pamela (*gently*) No-one deserves to die, Derek.

Derek She did. (*Bitterly*) Caroline Faye.

Pamela (*puzzled*) Who?

Lionel (*dismissively*) Woman he thought she was. But he'd got his wires crossed. It wasn't her at all.

Derek (*puzzled*) What wasn't?

Lionel (*to him*) The old girl. She wasn't Caroline Faye. Joanie got it wrong. Case of mistaken identity.

Derek (*rising in confusion*) But it couldn't have been. She said so. She said she'd know her anywhere.

Lionel (*smirking*) That's my Joanie. Likes to think she's infallible. (*Amused*) But she spat bloody feathers when she found out the real Faye woman popped her clogs last year. Best laugh I've had in ages.

Derek (*staring at him in dismay*) You're lying.

Lionel (*harshly*) I'd watch my tongue if I were you. I don't do lying. If there's anything I want to say, I bloody well say it. No beating round the bushes.

Derek (*stricken*) But if she wasn't Caroline Faye, an innocent woman's dead. (*Confused*) She told me to leave it to her. That she'd take care of everything.

Pamela and Lionel exchange puzzled glances

Pamela Who did?
Derek (*explosively*) Mother, of course. (*He lets out a moan of anguish*)

Pamela and Lionel exchange looks again

Pamela (*gently*) Your mother's dead, Derek.
Derek (*hotly*) Of course she's dead. Do you think I don't know? Did you think I'd forgotten? I'm not stupid, you know. (*More in control*) But it doesn't mean she can't talk to me. We always talked. (*Glaring at Pamela; fiercely*) And we still do. (*Retreating into himself*) What have I done?
Lionel (*with distaste*) He's nutty as a fruit cake.
Pamela (*rising*) Shut up. (*To Derek*) You haven't done anything, Derek. No-one has. (*She moves* UC) It doesn't matter who you thought Mrs Pike was, her death was an accident. She slipped and fell.
Derek (*shaking his head*) She didn't. She didn't. She was murdered.
Pamela (*firmly*) No, Derek.
Derek (*insistently*) I saw him do it. As I crossed the stepping stones. That's why I lost my footing. I was too busy watching him.
Pamela (*thrown*) Who?
Derek The Harlequin. Jemmy Junkins.

Pamela looks at Derek in disbelief

Lionel (*to Pamela, scornfully*) What did I tell you? He's off his bloody rocker.

Pamela throws Lionel a vicious glance

Pamela (*to Derek: gently*) What makes you think it was Jemmy you saw?
Derek (*forcefully*) Because it was. He was wearing his costume. The one in the painting. (*His concentration drifts away as he pictures it again*) Green — and red — and yellow — and blue.
Pamela (*cautiously*) And ... what was he doing?
Derek (*in another world*) Standing there. Standing in the snow with the flakes dancing round him. (*Revitalized*) Then she came round the corner with her head down and almost bumped into him. She must have known he was going to kill her because she threw her arm up and staggered back.

But he moved like lightning. Before she could run, he grabbed her coat and
swung her into the wall as hard as he could. That's when I fell in the water.
By the time I got up again, she was dead.

Pamela (*after a moment*) And where was Jemmy?

Derek (*shaking his head*) Gone.

Lionel turns away in disgust

Pamela (*carefully*) You didn't tell the *police* this?

Derek (*distantly*) I didn't tell anybody. I thought she was Caroline Faye and
I wanted her dead. She deserved it for all the pain she'd caused.

Pamela reaches out to him, but he recoils

(*Agitatedly*) I wanted to kill her myself, but Mother wouldn't hear of it.
"You don't lay a finger on her," she said. "I'll take care of it." (*Dismayed*)
But she's killed the wrong woman. (*He moans and gnaws at his knuckles*)

Lionel Make your mind up. A few seconds ago she was brained by Jimmy
bloody Jampots, or whatever his name is. Now you're telling us your
mother did it. Who'll it be next? Laurel and Hardy?

Derek (*hotly*) She must have asked him to help her.

Lionel (*scoffing*) Help her? You're the one needs help, sunshine. You want
putting away for your own good.

Pamela (*sharply*) Leave him alone, can't you? He's in shock. He doesn't
know what he's saying.

Lionel No. And nor does any other bugger. (*He finishes his drink*)

Pamela He needs to lie down. (*To Derek*) Let me help you upstairs.

Derek (*protesting*) But I've got to find Mother. I've got to tell her.

Pamela When you've had a rest.

Derek (*explosively*) No. I need to find her now.

Derek flings the chair violently backwards and races out of the room

(*Calling*) Mother, Mother.

Pamela (*calling after him*) Derek. (*Turning to Lionel, concerned*) He's
going outside.

Lionel (*sourly*) Best place for him. He's round the bloody twist.

Pamela (*fiercely*) He hasn't a coat on. He'll freeze to death.

Lionel (*unconcerned*) One less lunatic to worry about. (*He sits in the chair*
DL)

Pamela glares at him, then hurries out

Sally (*off*) Pammy …

Pamela (*off; calling*) Back in a minute. Don't lock up. I'm borrowing this.

Sally enters the room, looking tired and on edge

Sally (*glancing around*) You've not seen a bottle of tablets, have you? I can't think what I've done with them.
Lionel (*pointedly*) Not for indigestion, are they?
Sally (*forcing a smile*) No. Just something I seem to have lost. (*Frowning*) You're not *having* tummy problems, are you?
Lionel (*drily*) In a manner of speaking. I'd not intended mentioning the matter right now, but as you ask, I may as well get it over with. I presume there'll be some sort of discount for tonight's inconvenience? (*He puts his empty glass on the chair arm*) I mean — it's not exactly what you advertised in the brochure, is it? An over-cooked dinner, one of the guests with her head bashed in and the local constabulary grilling the rest of us like we were common criminals.
Sally (*taken aback*) I'm sure they were ——
Lionel (*cutting her off*) And then there's the bloody madman in the room next to ours. Moaning and groaning half the night and keeping decent folks awake. (*Rising*) We thought this were a guest house, Mrs Lockwood. Not a private asylum. In my opinion, the least you can do is offer reasonable compensation. Wouldn't look good in the papers, now, would it?
Sally (*flustered*) I'll — have a word with Bryan.
Lionel I mean ... it's not exactly cheap here, is it? And when you're paying that sort of money, you expect consideration. Fifty per cent off the bill'd make a start, to my way of thinking. (*He heads for the door, then pauses*) Oh — and I'd like a bottle of that red sent up to the room if you wouldn't mind. On the house, of course. (*Affably*) Good-night.

Lionel exits

Sally remains dumbstruck for a second, then takes a deep breath to steady herself before moving down to the chair to pick up the glass

Isobel enters, looking pale and unsteady. She has a blanket draped around her shoulders and clutches it to her

Sally Miss Clarke ... (*She moves rapidly towards Isobel*)
Isobel (*forcing a smile*) It's all right. I look worse than I feel.
Sally I thought you were *sleeping*. (*She puts her arm around Isobel's shoulders*) He said you'd be out for hours. (*She moves Isobel down to the settee*)
Isobel (*wanly*) Never believe a doctor.

Sally (*concerned*) You look awful. (*She seats her*) Are you sure you're all right?

Isobel (*nodding*) Just the shock. I'd never seen a body before. And all that blood.

Sally (*hastily*) Yes. Well you don't want to talk about that.

Isobel (*weakly*) I can't believe I had hysterics. I feel so stupid.

Sally (*firmly*) There's nothing to feel stupid about. I'd have done exactly the same if I'd found her. (*Concerned*) Would you like a hot water bottle? You're cold as ice.

Isobel Probably the sedative. I'm not very good with medicines.

Sally (*fussing*) You should have stayed upstairs. Given it time to wear off. But a cup of strong tea with plenty of sugar won't go amiss. It may be old-fashioned, but it'll do you the world of good. Just stay where you are and I'll be back in a jiffy. (*She moves towards the door*)

Isobel (*anxiously*) Do they know yet who did it?

Sally (*turning back*) Oh, no. No. It wasn't what we thought, thank goodness ... No-one attacked her. It was an accident. She slipped in the snow and fell against the wall.

Isobel (*relieved*) Thank God for that.

Sally (*sighing*) Not that it's any less tragic. (*Briskly*) I'll get you that tea.

Sally exits

Isobel pulls the blanket tighter and leans back, closing her eyes

A moment later, Pamela enters, looking frozen and closing an umbrella sprinkled with snowflakes

Pamela (*shaking the umbrella*) It's no use. I've lost him. (*She sees Isobel*) What are you doing here?

Isobel (*wanly*) That's the second time you've asked me that.

Pamela (*moving* DS) I thought you'd be out of it till breakfast. He gave you enough Valium to fell an elephant. (*Grudgingly*) How are you feeling? (*She props the umbrella behind the settee*)

Isobel (*drily*) Like a felled elephant.

Pamela (*embarrassed*) Sorry about the slap. I was trying to calm you down.

Isobel What's a broken jaw between friends? (*Curiously*) Where've you been?

Pamela Looking for Derek. If anyone needs a doctor it's him. God knows what's going on inside his head.

Isobel (*sitting up*) Why? What's happened?

Pamela I'll explain later. But it's given me an idea. (*She glances over her shoulder at the doorway, then lowers her voice*) How far away's the car?

Isobel I told you. About a mile up the road.

Pamela (*sitting on the settee arm*) And how bad is it? Can it be driven?

Isobel I suppose so. Once it's out of the ditch. It's not damaged, or anything ...

Pamela Then I'm going for the stuff tonight. Before it's too late. Give me the keys and I'll leave it in the boot.

Isobel (*protesting*) You can't. Not in this.

Pamela (*insisting*) I've got to. We can't leave it there. It'll be days before it clears.

Isobel I'll pick it up tomorrow. After they've towed me out.

Pamela And what about the tracks you'd leave? They'd be visible for miles. (*Patiently*) It'll be two foot deep, come daylight.

Isobel (*acidly*) And you'll just float above it, will you?

Pamela (*rising and moving* DR) If I get it now, any tracks'll be covered before farmers start checking their sheep. And even if they're not, folk round here are used to seeing me striding the hills — no matter what the weather. They won't question it if they hear I've been searching for Derek. It's the perfect cover. Providing we make use of it.

Isobel (*frowning*) So where's he gone?

Pamela (*drily*) It won't matter if we don't find him soon. He'll freeze to death up there. It's bitter. (*After a hesitation*) I'd better tell Sally.

Sally enters behind her carrying a cup of tea on a saucer

Sally Tell me what? (*She moves down to the settee*)

Pamela (*turning to Sally*) It's Derek. He's thrown a wobbly and headed for the hills.

Sally (*stunned*) Oh, no.

Pamela I followed him to the stepping stones but lost him on the other side. He's not even wearing a coat.

Sally (*concerned*) I knew there was something wrong with him. He's not been the same since ... I'd better get Bryan. (*She thrusts the cup of tea at Isobel and turns to leave*)

Pamela (*quickly*) It's all right. I've got my gear upstairs — and he can't avoid leaving tracks.

Sally (*protesting*) But you can't go on your own. Not if ——

Pamela He's not dangerous. A bit disturbed, that's all. It won't take him long to calm down. Not in this lot. Have you a torch I can borrow?

Sally (*distractedly*) There's one in the kitchen.

Pamela (*briskly*) I'll be down in five minutes.

Pamela hurries out

Isobel (*to Sally*) It's like a nightmare, isn't it? First Mrs Pike. And now this.

Sally suddenly bursts into tears and sits in the armchair UR

(*Startled*) Here. Here. (*She puts her tea on the settee arm, rises quickly and moves to Sally*) It's *not that* bad. (*She kneels beside her*) If anyone can find him, it's Pammy.

Sally (*sobbing*) I can't *take* any more.

Isobel (*soothingly*) I know it's been dreadful today, but none of it's your fault.

Sally (*still sobbing*) Everything we had. Every penny. If we lose this, we've got nothing.

Isobel (*blankly*) Lose it?

Sally (*despairingly*) The *Harlequin*. We're never going to own it. I knew it all along. It wasn't meant. (*She sobs*)

Isobel (*gently*) I don't understand.

Bryan enters. He wears his chef's jacket and trousers

Bryan (*with quiet dignity*) We're having a few problems.

Isobel stands and backs towards the settee as he moves down to comfort Sally

(*To Sally; gently*) It's all right, love. We can ride it out. It's nothing we can't cope with.

Sally (*bitterly*) We shouldn't have to cope. We shouldn't. (*She sobs harder*)

Bryan (*attempting to raise her to her feet*) Let's get you upstairs. I'll finish off down here.

Sally (*resisting weakly*) I don't want to go upstairs.

Bryan (*lifting her*) Yes, you do. A night's rest'll do you the world of good. It'll all look better in the morning.

Isobel sits on the settee. Sally continues to sob

Isobel (*hesitantly*) Is there anything I can help with ?

Bryan We'll be fine, thanks. Nothing to worry about.

Isobel picks up her tea

Joan, looking peeved, limps in and moves c, *behind the settee*

Joan (*tartly*) Is there anything that works in this place? It's bad enough we've to hang out of the bedroom window to get a phone signal. Now we have to freeze to death. I'm a sick woman — in case you hadn't heard.

Bryan (*glancing at her*) I'll attend to you in a moment, Mrs Reece.

Joan (*snapping*) You'll attend to me now. We booked a room here, not a
flaming refrigerator. And if something's not done about warming it up,
p.d.q., you can whistle for your money. (*She glowers at Bryan*)

Isobel (*helpfully*) Have you checked the thermostat?

Joan Of course we have. We're not stupid. You can see your own breath in
there.

Bryan (*soothingly*) I'll see what the problem is as soon as I've dealt with
Sally.

Joan (*heavily*) We know what the problem is. We want *a solution*. (*Looking
at Sally suspiciously*) What's wrong with her?

Bryan She's not feeling too well.

Joan (*acidly*) Probably food poisoning. I've done nothing but throw up
myself since that salmon I had for dinner.

Sally (*wrenching free of Bryan*) There was nothing wrong with the salmon,
Mrs Reece. And if you think you've been poisoned, you'd better examine
your tongue. It's highly possible you've bitten it.

Sally storms out of the room

Joan gapes in shock

Bryan (*apologetically*) I'm sorry about that.

Joan (*seething*) I should think you are. It's not enough we're treated like dog-
muck: now we have insults. (*She moves towards Bryan*) If there was any
chance of leaving this — hell-hole — tonight, we'd be packing the cases
now. (*Grimly*) But I'll tell you this much for nothing. First thing tomorrow,
we're out of here. Even if we have to ski to flamin' Buxton. (*She turns to
exit*)

Bryan (*anxiously*) There's no need for that, Mrs Reece. If there are problems,
we'll obviously do our utmost to solve them.

Joan pauses

But as you'll appreciate, everyone's deeply shocked by Mrs Pike's death
and it's hit Sally harder than most. Give us a little time and I assure you that
Christmas'll be the best one you've ever had.

Joan (*turning back*) Not if we've frozen to death before it gets here.

Bryan (*hastily*) There's no chance of that. I'll look at your heating now, and
if it can't be fixed, we'll move you to another room. (*He smiles hopefully*)

Joan (*her eyes narrowing*) And what about something decent to eat? You
can hardly claim tonight's effort passed for dinner.

Bryan I could do omelettes. Or sandwiches. Roast beef? Ham? Anything
you like.

There is a moment's silence as Joan considers

Joan How about cheese?

Bryan (*a little surprised*) Well—yes. I can do cheese if you'd prefer. We've quite a good selection. If there's any particular ...?

Joan Not if it's real cheese. (*Sharply*) But we don't want that rubbery muck with mouse-holes in it. (*As an afterthought*) Or cream cheese. Something with a bite to it. And plenty of pickle.

Bryan (*relieved*) I'll sort out the heating first, and do them as soon as I've finished.

Joan (*flatly*) We'll have the sandwiches first if you don't mind. That way we don't die of starvation while we're waiting for the ice to melt. (*She limps towards the door*)

Isobel (*noticing the limp*) Something wrong with your foot?

Joan (*scowling*) Burst blister. (*Bitterly*) Another side-benefit of country living.

Bryan (*quickly*) Can I get you a dressing? There's a first aid box down the hall.

Joan (*acidly*) But no plasters in it, and precious little else. Thank God I've not broken a leg. You'd have probably tried to set it with cocktail sticks.

Joan exits

Bryan exhales loudly

Isobel Take a deep breath and count to ten slowly.

Bryan (*distractedly*) Sorry?

Isobel (*kindly*) How do you do it? Put up with people like her?

Bryan (*forcing a smile*) Years of practice — and not forgetting the tradesman's motto: the customer's always right.

Isobel (*drily*) But not always right in the head. If I were in your shoes, I'd have tossed her into the snow like Little Orphan Annie.

Bryan (*mildly*) Then perhaps it's a good thing you're not. (*Remembering*) Is there anything I can get for you, Miss Clarke?

Isobel Still got my tea, thanks. (*She indicates the cup and saucer*) And I couldn't eat a thing. Not after ... (*Correcting herself*) Not till breakfast, anyway.

Pamela enters, now wearing her outdoor clothing and boots and carrying a small knapsack

Pamela (*as she enters*) Just need the torch and I'll be off.

Bryan looks at her in surprise

(*Seeing Bryan's look*) Don't worry. We'll be back before you know it. He won't have got far. He's more used to roads than hills and he's not exactly dressed for Winter Olympics. I wouldn't be surprised if he's changed his mind already.

Bryan (*blankly*) What are you talking about?

Pamela Sorry. I thought you knew. (*Explaining*) It's Derek. He's had some sort of breakdown and gone to join the fairies. I'm just going after him.

Bryan (*hastily*) I'll get my coat.

Isobel (*quickly*) Don't forget the Reeces.

Bryan They'll have to wait. (*To Pamela*) I'll be with you in half a minute.

Pamela (*shaking her head*) No need. I can follow his tracks easily. And he's less likely to do anything stupid if he sees it's only me doing the chasing. Besides — he might circle round and be back before I catch up with him, and someone should be here to handle him.

Isobel I *do* think that's best, Mr Lockwood.

Bryan (*uncertainly*) If you're sure?

Pamela (*nodding*) If I can't find him, we'll do a re-think. But at the moment, I'm better off on my own. There's a thermal blanket in here (*she indicates the knapsack*) plus a few odds and ends, so if I could have that torch ...

Bryan (*doubtfully*) It's only a small one.

Pamela Better than a box of matches. (*She puts the knapsack down*)

Bryan I'll get it for you, now.

Bryan exits

Isobel (*hissing*) You're not really going to look for him?

Pamela (*moving R of the settee*) Of course I am. We don't want another corpse on the doorstep. But I'll pick up the stuff first. An hour or so's not going to make that much difference.

Isobel (*protesting*) It'll take you an hour to get to the car.

Pamela (*sharply*) Then he's going to be damned uncomfortable till I find him. I'm not risking my neck by having you floundering about in broad daylight. You've caused enough problems as it is.

Isobel (*bridling*) Well, thank you.

Pamela Give me the keys. (*She holds out her hand*)

Isobel (*sourly*) They're up in the room. I don't carry them round like magic talismans.

Pamela (*pointedly*) Then if you wouldn't mind ...

Isobel (*irritatedly; rising*) Wait at the foot of the stairs. I'll throw 'em down to you.

Pamela And try to do it discreetly.

Isobel (*bitterly*) Yes, Miss.

Isobel pushes past Pamela and exits

Pamela sighs deeply and leans on the armchair

A moment later Bryan enters carrying a small torch

Bryan Best I can manage, I'm afraid. (*He hands the torch to Pamela*) Look. Are you *sure* you want to do this?
Pamela (*wryly*) I can't say I want to, but the sooner he's back here, the better. There's not even a sheep pen in that direction. (*She tests the torch*)
Bryan (*concerned*) Should I call Dr Lewins?
Pamela You wouldn't get thanked if you did. Even what's-his-name, the policeman, got it in the neck when he dragged her here to look at Mrs Pike. She was on her way to the centre's annual "do" when the call went through and wasn't best pleased about it. (*She smiles*) Let's see what he's like when I find him. He may need psychiatric help more than the physical kind.
Bryan (*frowning*) You're not serious?
Pamela (*wryly*) He thinks he saw Jemmy attack Mrs Pike.

Bryan looks startled

I said he was off with the fairies. Let's hope the cold's snapped him out of it.

Sally enters with a small covered tray of sandwiches. She has pulled herself together, but is obviously in a state of tension

Sally (*to Bryan; tight-lipped*) Sandwiches. (*She thrusts the tray at him*) And you needn't worry. I've not poisoned them. Though God knows what stopped me.
Bryan (*reprovingly*) Sally.
Sally If it hadn't been for her and her "mistaken identity", none of this would have happened. (*To Pamela, anxiously*) You will find him, won't you?
Pamela Of course I will. He may be frozen to the marrow, but he's going to be safe. Scout's Honour. (*Smiling*) I'll just spend a penny, then make myself scarce.

Pamela exits into the hall, slipping the torch into her pocket

Bryan (*to Sally*) And I'll take these up. (*He prepares to exit*)
Sally (*stopping him; doubtfully*) Do you think we can? Survive, I mean.
Bryan (*after a slight hesitation*) We'll talk about it later.
Sally I need to know now, Bryan. (*She turns away, on the verge of tears*) I can't go on like this. I can't.
Bryan We'll get Christmas out of the way and see if ——

Sally (*subsiding into the armchair*) They won't, Bryan. You know they won't. We're going to lose it. It's over.

Bryan Look. Let me take these to the Reeces and see what's wrong with their heating — if anything. We'll talk when I come back down.

Sally (*bitterly*) There isn't any point. We're finished.

Bryan No.

Sally (*hotly*) Of course we are. We're barely covering costs.

Bryan (*insistently*) It's going to get better.

Sally (*bitterly*) You've been saying that for the last five years. But it hasn't done, has it? It hasn't.

Bryan (*reasonably*) It takes time, Sal. Look at the New Year bookings. And the ones for Easter. They're the best we've ever had.

Sally And how long do you think we'll keep them when this gets out? They'll be cancelling left, right and centre.

Bryan It's hardly headline news, Sal. An accident in the snow. Who can blame us for that? (*Uncomfortably*) Look — I've got to get these upstairs. Keeping the gruesome twosome happy's the main thing to worry about at the moment. Stop them blabbing their mouths off and this'll all be forgotten by the end of the year.

Sally (*turning away*) Not by me, it won't.

Bryan tries to think of something to say, but fails. He turns to exit

Pamela enters and crosses to her knapsack

Pamela (*cheerfully*) Wish me luck.

Bryan (*uneasily*) Just — watch what you're doing.

Pamela Don't worry. I could teach Eskimos a thing or two. (*She picks up the knapsack*) Right. (*Mock-heroically*) "I may be some time" as Captain Oates once said. (*She grins*)

Bryan (*rolling his eyes*) Yes. Famous last words, I believe.

Bryan exits

Pamela (*to Sally*) You might want to slip a hot water bottle in his bed, Sal. He could be hypothermic by the time we make it back. (*She moves towards the door*)

Sally (*suddenly*) Pammy ...

Pamela halts

(*Rising; anxiously*) You're sure you can find him? (*She moves to Pamela*) You're not just *saying* it?

Pamela (*surprised*) A blind man could follow him. Now stop worrying. I've got my mobile and the minute he's bundled up, I'll give you a call. It's not a bad signal once you're past the tree line.

Sally And what if he's still — disturbed?

Pamela (*soothingly*) We'll cross that bridge when we get to it. But if you ask my opinion, he'll be so glad to see me and my little goody-bag, he'll fall on his knees and ask me to marry him. (*Archly*) Not that I'd dream of accepting. I'd enough trouble with husband number one. He was into spirits, too. But his came in bottles. (*She grins*) Onwards and upwards.

Pamela exits

Sally stands gazing after her for a moment, then drifts to the table, scrapes up the half-finished jigsaw puzzle and puts the pieces back in the box. She moves DR *and turns down the thermostat on the radiator. About to leave the room she notices the teacup and saucer on the settee arm and picks them up. She glances around for a final check*

Bryan slowly enters the room, a puzzled look on his face and a sheet of paper in his hand

Sally (*noticing him*) Have you fixed it?

Bryan (*distractedly*) No. No. It's definitely up the spout. Not even lukewarm. We'll have to move them out and call Jenson's. (*He stares at the paper*)

Sally (*frowning*) What *is* it?

Bryan (*still puzzled*) It doesn't make sense.

Sally What doesn't?

Bryan I thought we could put them in Columbine — Mrs Pike's old room — so I opened it up to see what needed moving and found this on the bedside table. (*He shows Sally the sheet of paper*)

Sally (*puzzled*) What is it?

Bryan A family tree. She was working on a family tree.

Sally (*still puzzled*) What's wrong with that? Everyone's at it, these days. It's almost a national craze.

Bryan You don't understand. It's not her family tree she's been working on. It's yours.

Sally (*surprised*) Mine?

Bryan (*handing her the sheet of paper*) And according to this — the pair of you were somehow related.

Sally looks at the paper in bewilderment

CURTAIN

SCENE 2

The same. Two hours later

The teacup, saucer and jigsaw puzzle have gone but otherwise the room is unchanged

When the CURTAIN *rises Sally is slumped on the settee, fast asleep, the family tree chart still clutched in her hand.*

There is a moment's pause

Isobel, enters, looking worried, wrapped in a dressing-gown. Seeing Sally, she stops in her tracks, uncertainly

Isobel (*softly*) Mrs Lockwood?

There is no reaction. Isobel hesitantly moves behind the settee

Mrs Lockwood?

There is still no response. Isobel straightens, bites her lip in indecision, then turns to leave

Bryan enters, a mug of coffee in each hand

Bryan (*startled*) Miss Clarke. (*He smiles nervously*) We thought you'd gone to bed. (*He notices Sally is asleep*)
Isobel (*apologetically*) I thought I heard a noise.
Bryan Noise?
Isobel In Pammy's room. (*Explaining*) I was half-asleep at the time and thought I'd dreamed it. But then I heard it again — and thinking she was back, went round to see how she'd done. (*Puzzled*) But the light was off and there wasn't a sign of her.
Bryan (*shaking his head*) She's still out there. We've been waiting for her to call. (*Concerned*) It's nearly midnight. If we don't hear soon, I'm going out after her.
Isobel (*hastily*) She'll be fine. I know she will. She knows the area like the back of her hand. (*Remembering*) She told me so — just before dinner.
Bryan (*not convinced*) But it all looks different under a foot of snow. And now it's drifting ... (*Proffering a mug*) Do you fancy a coffee? Looks like Sal's out of it and I'd rather not wake her. She could do with the rest.

Isobel (*taking the mug*) Thanks. (*Changing the subject*) So what do you think it *was*? The noise I heard. (*She sips at the coffee*)

Bryan (*perching on the arm of the easy chair, R*) Probably floorboards. They do creak a bit, being originals. The ones in our room still make us jump — and this is our fifth year. (*He sips at his coffee*)

Isobel (*shaking her head*) It was more furtive than that. It was almost like — like someone trying not to make a noise.

Bryan (*puzzled*) Well, I can't think who. There's only the Reeces upstairs at present and I can't see what they'd want in Pammy's room. Especially if it involved anything furtive. (*Remembering*) By the way — we've moved them across the hall, so they shouldn't disturb you if another fight breaks out.

Isobel (*sympathetically*) I thought you must have. I heard them talking when I came out of my room. (*Correcting herself*) Well — she was talking. He was having a coughing fit.

Bryan (*groaning theatrically*) Don't say he's caught a cold. If he has, it's bound to be our fault. Come the morning, he'll be laid up with double pneumonia or Avian flu from the Toilet Duck. And how much'll that cost us?

Isobel (*smiling*) They're certainly an odd couple.

Bryan (*grimly*) I could think of a better description. (*Standing*) Look — I wonder if you'd mind waiting here in case Sal wakes up? I'll only be a minute or so. (*Explaining*) I want to slip outside and see if there's any sign of them. They must be heading back by this time.

Isobel You won't see far in this. And she did say she'd call.

Bryan (*uncomfortably*) I know. But I've got to do something. I can't just sit here twiddling my thu ... (*He whips round suddenly to face the door*) Hang on. (*Rising swiftly*) Thank the Lord for that. They've made it. (*He thrusts his coffee mug into her hand and moves towards the door*)

Isobel (*blankly*) I didn't hear ...

Bryan Wake Sally.

Bryan hurries out

Isobel quickly puts down the mugs and leans over the settee to gently shake Sally

Isobel Mrs Lockwood ...

Sally (*drowsily*) Hmm? (*She wakes with a start and sits up, dropping the family tree chart to the floor. Disorientated*) What is it? What's wrong?

Isobel It's Pammy and Mr Tyndale. They're back. Your husband's gone to meet them.

Sally (*struggling to her feet*) I must have been asleep. What time is it?

Isobel Nearly midnight.
Sally (*anxiously*) Is everything all right?
Isobel I've no idea. They've not come in, yet.
Sally I'll run a hot bath for him.

Sally hurries out

Isobel moves to the doorway, looking out

Bryan (*off*) Here we are. Watch the door.
Pamela (*off; panting*) Where do you want him?
Bryan (*off*) Upstairs, I think. Get him under the duvet.
Isobel (*to them*) Mrs Lockwood's running a bath for him.
Bryan (*off*) Up the stairs it is, then. I'll take him from here, Pammy. Help
   yourself to a brandy or something. You look like you need it. Come on,
   Derek. Soon have you warm again.

Isobel steps back

   *Pamela enters, exhausted, taking off her gloves. Snow is on her cap, jacket,
   trousers and boots*

Isobel (*anxiously: sotto voce*) Have you done it ? Did you *get* there ?
Pamela (*moving heavily* DR) What do you think ? (*Removing her cap and
   shaking it*) It's in the boot.
Isobel (*relieved*) And you're sure nobody saw you ?

Pamela gives Isobel an irritated glance

   I mean — you've been out there for hours. I was starting to think ——
Pamela (*cutting in*) I said I'd do it and I did. The rest's up to you.
Isobel (*snapping*) There's no need to be snotty about it. I didn't crash on
   purpose.
Pamela (*distractedly*) I know you didn't. But I'm cold. I'm tired and I've just
   realized something that's knocked me for six. (*She sinks into the armchair*)
Isobel (*frowning*) What is it ? (*She moves closer to Pamela*)
Pamela (*shaking her head*) Not now, Izzy.
Isobel Is it to do with us ? What we're doing here ?
Pamela (*irritated*) I've just told you. I need to think about it.
Isobel (*tightly*) But if it affects me, I want to know. I'm not spending the next
   few years in Holloway for anybody. Let alone Frankie Allen. We're the
   ones taking risks while he swans round in his roller, raking in the profit.

Pamela (*tiredly*) It's nothing to do with us. Or Frank Allen. (*Pointedly*) And you'd do well remembering if it wasn't for him, we'd have nothing to take risks for.

Isobel (*sulkily*) He could still afford to pay us better. It's peanuts compared to what he gets out of it. (*She moves* L, *behind the settee*)

Pamela And how would you know?

Isobel (*sharply*) Because I'm not as trusting as you are. (*Smugly*) Before I pass everything on, I have a friend round to give it the once-over.

Pamela looks at her in horror

(*Firmly*) And according to him, we're being ripped off every run we do.

Pamela You idiot. (*Rising*) You brainless, brainless — idiot.

Isobel (*shrugging*) P'raps I am — but I'm still smarter than Frankie gives me credit for. (*Smirking*) Two can play his little game.

Pamela (*suspiciously*) And what's that supposed to mean? (*Suddenly alarmed*) What have you done?

Isobel (*snapping*) Nothing I shouldn't have done six months ago. (*Easily*) Simply "lose" a couple of items from each shipment before it leaves the country, and do a private deal with someone who doesn't ask questions ...

Pamela (*stunned*) You mean — you're ripping him off? Frank Allen? (*She turns away in disbelief*) Oh, my God. He'll have your guts for garters. (*She sinks into the chair again*)

Isobel (*moving back* R) And how'll he find out? Will you tell him? (*Perching on the settee arm*) Look — I know we don't always see eye to eye, but we're a good team, you and me. Without us, the whole network'd shut down.

Pamela (*acidly*) Don't flatter yourself. He was running this scam before you were out of your nappies.

Isobel All the more reason for looking to the future. He's eighty years old if he's a day and can't go on much longer. And where's it leave us when he does snuff it? I'll tell you. Up the creek without a paddle in sight. (*She rises*)

Pamela (*snapping*) You won't need a paddle, dearie. You'll be at the bottom of the creek with your feet in a block of concrete.

Isobel (*amused*) Spare me the melodrama. He's not exactly "The Godfather", is he?

Pamela (*gritting her teeth*) You don't know what he is. And you wouldn't want to find out, believe me. Just drop whatever you're playing at and deliver the stuff as agreed. That way, you might live long enough to draw your old age pension.

Isobel (*moving* L) I'm quaking in my boots.

Pamela Well, don't say you haven't been *warned*.

Sally enters carrying Derek's shirt and trousers and Isobel's blood-stained jacket

Sally (*relieved*) He hasn't got frostbite, thank goodness, but we'd better call the doctor, first thing. I'm sure he needs stitches. He's bleeding quite badly.
Pamela (*frowning*) Bleeding?
Sally From his cheek. The heat's started it off again. I'll have to soak his things to get the worst out. (*Sighing*) Still — they can go in with Bryan's top. How he didn't *scald* himself, I'll never know. It was absolutely boiling, that gravy. (*To Isobel*) I've got your jacket, too, Miss Clarke. (*She indicates it*) I'll do what I can with it, but you'll need a professional cleaner's help for best results. I hope it wasn't *too* expensive.
Isobel (*hastily*) I shouldn't bother. I couldn't wear it again. Not knowing her blood'd been all over it.
Sally I'll do what I can, anyway. Perhaps you could give it to a charity shop? I'm sure they'd welcome it with open arms. Oh ... And I've left your letter on the bedside table. Lucky there was none on that or you'd have had to write it again. (*She turns to exit*)
Isobel (*puzzled*) Letter?
Sally (*after a pause*) The one I found in your pocket. Good job I checked. I left a ball-point pen in mine once. (*She rolls her eyes*) Never again.

Sally exits

Pamela (*drily*) I'm surprised you found time to write. (*She unfastens her jacket*)
Isobel I didn't. I picked it up outside. Just before I found Mrs Pike. I thought she must have dropped it, and stuck it in my pocket when I saw her by the wall. I'd totally forgotten it ...
Pamela You should have handed it to the police.
Isobel (*patiently*) How could I? I was pumped full of Valium. Remember? (*Shrugging*) Anyway I can hand it in when I go to the station. I'm supposed to be making a statement first thing tomorrow.
Pamela (*curiously*) So who was she writing to?
Isobel Why?
Pamela They'll be in for a shock when they get it.
Isobel (*thinking*) Daughter, I think. She mentioned the name before she went out. Aileen something-or-other. (*Remembering*) Merrill. That was it. Aileen Merrill.
Pamela (*sitting up*) Are you sure about that?
Isobel Not entirely. I'm not particularly interested in other people's correspondence, but I think that's what it said. Why'd you ask?

Pamela (*fretting*) Because just before you found her, there was a woman on the line trying to reach her. Remember? By the time the fuss died down, she must have given up and rung off. Bryan tried to call back later, after the police had gone, but all he got was a message saying the office was closed for business till January.

Isobel So?

Pamela (*heavily*) It happened to be a solicitor's office. Merrill and Jackson in Curzon Street.

Isobel (*blankly*) And?

Pamela (*frustratedly*) I don't know. It's just I always get the jitters when coincidence starts rearing its ugly little head. Why would you write to your solicitor a few days before Christmas, when you could easily phone them?

Isobel (*moving further* L) I could think of a thousand reasons. But if it really worries you, we can easily find out. (*She notices the family tree chart and picks it up*) It wouldn't be the first time I'd steamed a letter open. (*Smugly*) You could ask my ex-husband.

Pamela (*noticing the chart*) What's that?

Isobel (*glancing at it idly*) Family tree.

Pamela Yours?

Isobel (*amused*) I know all I want to know about my background, thank you very much. No. It's our esteemed hostess's. The lovely Mrs L.

Pamela Sally's? (*She holds out her hand for it*)

Isobel (*moving to her*) Nice writing, I must say. (*She holds it out to Pamela*) Mine always looks like I've used a spider dipped in an inkwell. (*She frowns and pulls back the chart*) Hang on. I've seen this *before*. (*She looks closely at the writing*)

Pamela What?

Isobel The writing. It's the same as on Mrs Pike's letter. (*She displays the chart*) Look at the way she's dotted the Is. With a circle, not a dot. And the cross-strokes on the Ts. It's Mrs Pike's chart.

Pamela (*taking it from her*) Then what's it doing down here? (*She scans it rapidly then lowers it, looking shaken*) Oh, my God.

Isobel (*concerned*) What is it? What's wrong?

Pamela (*almost to herself*) It might be the reason she died. (*Looking up*) The letter. I need to *see* it.

Isobel stares at her

Hurry.

Isobel If you'll tell me what's going on ...

Pamela (*jumping up*) Don't bother. I'll get it myself.

Pamela drops the chart on the chair and hurries towards the door

Sally enters with a small tray on which are two steaming mugs

Pamela and Sally almost collide

Pamela exits

Sally (*startled*) Pammy? (*She looks out through the door after Pamela, then turns to Isobel, concerned*) Is something wrong?
Isobel (*lightly*) Urgent call from Mother Nature. Out in the cold too long ...
Sally (*relieved*) I thought you'd appreciate a warm drink. (*She puts the tray on the table behind the settee*) It's only hot chocolate, I'm afraid, but I've added a splash of Grand Marnier to liven it up. I think she deserves it, don't you? I don't know *what* we'd have done without her. (*She takes a mug and carries it to Isobel*)
Isobel (*accepting it*) That's what they all say.
Sally (*frowning*) Have you met before, then?
Isobel (*realizing her mistake*) Oh, no. No. It's just an expression. (*She smiles*) Must be a family thing. My sister uses it, too.
Sally (*ruefully*) I never had a sister. Two brothers, once. Older than me, (*reflectively*) but both gone now.
Isobel (*quickly*) Oh, I am sorry ...
Sally (*sitting on the settee and giving a tight smile*) Drowned in the Lake District. Back in the 1980s. Last of the line, me.
Isobel (*curiously*) Is that why Mrs Pike was researching your family tree?

Sally looks startled, Isobel picks up the chart and hands it to her

I found it on the floor. Couldn't help noticing.
Sally (*accepting it*) Oh, no. No. We've no idea what that's about. Bryan found it in her room — afterwards. (*Staring at the chart*) We can't understand it. According to this, we shared the same ancestor.
Isobel (*sitting in the armchair*) And you didn't know?
Sally Hadn't a clue. I mean — there was no resemblance. And she never said anything. She was just another guest. If only she'd mentioned it.
Isobel (*after a moment*) So what do you think she was doing here?
Sally We've no idea. I don't even know how she found me.
Isobel Depends how desperate she was. You've built up a reputation with this place, from what Pammy tells me. She could have been after money.
Sally (*bitterly*) Fat chance of that. We may look like we're rolling in it, but unless we have a miracle, we'll be on the market again within six months.
Isobel (*frowning*) You mentioned that earlier. But I didn't understand.
Sally (*with false brightness*) It's quite simple. We can't keep up with expenditure. And if we do cut back, we lose the very attraction that's made us what we are.

Isobel (*helpfully*) You could raise your prices.

Sally (*shaking her head*) We're already the highest priced guest house for miles. To charge even more'd be suicide. No. I'm afraid we're done for. It's the end of the road for us. And poor old Jemmy.

Isobel (*puzzled*) Who?

Sally (*forcing a smile*) Jemmy Junkins. It was his place, you see. The old coaching inn. He was the one who owned it. Not brother Victor. (*Dismissively*) He was only the landlord. No-one else knew, of course. Victor saw to that. As soon as he realized Jemmy would never walk again, he destroyed all the papers and took control of everything. And if it hadn't been for Marie Lloyd, none of it would ever have come to light.

Isobel looks bemused

She came to see him here. After his accident. Called in on her way back from Manchester. They'd known each other for years and Jemmy told her everything. Begged her to find Rosie and ask why she'd never been to visit him or answered his letters.

Isobel (*bewildered*) Rosie?

Sally Rose Pelham. A shop girl he'd met before he came to Derbyshire. She was only seventeen, but they'd fallen in love and were going to be married as soon as he got back to London. (*Bitterly*) Crippling himself put an end to that.

Isobel So she'd jilted him?

Sally (*fiercely*) She loved him till the day he died.

Isobel (*puzzled*) Then why ... ?

Sally Because scheming brother Victor never posted his letters. She didn't get any of them. For five years she thought she'd been abandoned. (*Bitterly*) It was a common enough story in those days. Love 'em and leave 'em and the Devil takes the consequence. Why should Jemmy be any different? He'd no idea what she'd gone through in the meantime. Thrown on the streets for shaming the family name, losing her job, and having to live in an East End slum with no money and a fatherless child to care for. (*She smiles fondly*) But Marie found her. Told her the truth, and even paid their fares to get them up here.

Isobel So they married after all?

Sally (*shaking her head*) Victor sent them packing. Called her a slut and threatened them with violence if they ever showed up again. They never even saw Jemmy, and went back to London in tears. A few months later he was dead.

Isobel And then what happened? Surely someone helped her? Marie Lloyd. Couldn't she have done something?

Sally I'm sure she would have, but she was on her way to New York. By the time she got back, it was all over. Jemmy was buried and Rose never saw her again.

Isobel (*curiously*) So how do you know all this?
Sally (*proudly*) Because Rose Pelham was my great-great-grandmother.
(*She smiles wanly*) We all knew the story, of course. Her descendants. But
what could we do? We'd no proof. Only word of mouth.

*Pamela enters unnoticed, looking tired. She has removed her outer jacket
and carries an opened letter*

Then when Mum died — six years ago — I realized when I was gone, too,
the story ended. We can't have a family — me and Bryan — and I wanted
so much to get back what rightfully belonged to us before it was too late.
Pamela (*quietly*) So you bought it. (*She stares at Sally intensely*)
Sally (*turning to her*) Pammy. I didn't hear you. There's hot chocolate on
the tray. (*Uncertainly*) What is it?
Pamela (*moving down between the others*) How long have you known, Sal?
Sally (*puzzled*) Known what?
Pamela (*conversationally*) Who she really was. When did you realize?
Before she arrived here, or afterwards?
Sally (*confused*) I don't know what you ...
Pamela Really? And you're willing to swear that, are you?
Isobel (*to Pamela*) What's wrong? What are you saying?
Pamela (*ignoring her*) I've read the letter, you see. (*She shows the others the
letter*) The one she was sending her solicitor. (*She moves slowly* L *in front
of the settee*) The only thing I don't know now, is why she had to die so
soon. Do you want to tell me that, Sal? Would you like to enlighten me?
(*She turns to look at Sally*)

Sally gapes at Pamela

Isobel (*to Pamela*) Are you out of your mind?
Pamela I don't think so. I'd be tempted to kill, myself, for a million pounds
or so.
Sally (*not understanding*) What?
Pamela It's what she was worth. She says so in the letter. And apart from
a donation to Cancer Research, you inherit the lot. Lock, stock and barrel.
Sally (*helplessly*) There must be some mistake.
Pamela Not according to this. (*She displays the letter again*) It's clear as
daylight. Would you like me to read it to you?
Isobel Pammy ...
Pamela (*reading*) "Dear Aileen, I was right. Mrs Lockwood is definitely
Rose's great-great-granddaughter. The resemblance is quite remarkable.
Change the hairstyle and clothing, and the two could be twins. How clever
of you to track her down for me. Now, of course, with all doubt removed,
my own great-grandmother, Violet Pelham, can rest in peace. To lose

contact with her elder sister at such a tender age, was a terrible blow. How fortunate times have changed and illegitimate children are no longer seen as a terrible disgrace. In view of the above, I presume the Trust she instated for Rose's descendants can now be wound up and Mrs Lockwood informed of her inheritance? With regard to my own will, everything remains as agreed: £500,000 to Cancer Research, and the remaining million or so to Mrs Lockwood, my only living relation. After further consideration, I have decided *not* to reveal the true purpose of my visit to Peak Lodge. To have the discovery of my existence followed in a matter of weeks by my demise would, I fear, be a bitter pill to swallow. Far better that the legacy should come unexpectedly. Don't you agree? Have a lovely time in Hastings and I look forward to seeing you again after Christmas. Yours sincerely, Marjory Pike." (*She lowers the letter*) Well?

Sally (*dazedly*) It's a joke.

Pamela Rather an expensive one. It cost the poor woman her life.

Isobel (*scornfully*) Don't be so stupid. Mrs Pike's death was an accident. Even the police agreed.

Bryan enters

Bryan Police agreed what? (*He glances from one to the other of the women*)

Isobel (*tightly*) That Mrs Pike's death was an accident.

Bryan Of course it was. We know that. (*Frowning*) Who says it wasn't?

Pamela (*flatly*) I do.

Sally (*rising and hurrying to Bryan*) She thinks I killed her.

Bryan puts his arm round Sally and looks at Pamela in surprise

Pamela No, I don't, Sal. You couldn't possibly have done it. You were inside with us. But you do know who did do it, don't you? (*She takes a deep breath*) It was Bryan.

Bryan (*shocked*) Me? (*He drops his arm*)

They all stare at Pamela

Pamela And you might have got away with it, if there hadn't been a witness.

Bryan (*giving a nervous laugh*) What are you talking about? What witness?

Pamela Derek Tyndale. He saw you attacking her. Just before he fell in the stream.

The others react

Bryan (*blustering*) That's ridiculous. I haven't attacked anyone. I was in the kitchen, for God's sake.

Pamela Not when she set off for the post box. You were waiting in the yard, weren't you, Bryan? He was in a highly emotional state and mistook you for Jemmy Junkins. Because of the colours, you see? Green and red and yellow and blue.

Sally (*relieved*) Then that proves it. You can't take Derek's word. He was having another breakdown. Bryan was in his whites. You saw him yourself. You said so. Going upstairs to change.

Pamela (*sadly*) And I also saw him outside — when he came to help me carry Derek in.

Isobel (*glowering*) Pammy ...

Pamela (*to her*) Remember the stained glass window on the landing? The light from it lit up the snow like a Harlequin suit — and he stepped straight into it.

There is a stunned silence

Sally (*confused*) Bryan?

Bryan (*hastily*) It's not what you're thinking, Sal. I didn't kill her. I was trying to help.

Pamela By trying to persuade her to give you the money, now?

Bryan (*puzzled*) Money? (*He glances at Sally*) What money?

Pamela You're telling me you didn't know? Come on, Bryan. I don't know how you found out, but it's the only way it makes sense. You don't kill a perfect stranger without having a reason.

Isobel (*uncertainly*) It's this place. Peak Lodge. The Harlequin. Whatever you want to call it. (*Rising*) It's losing money. She's just told me. They think they're going to lose it.

Pamela (*upset*) Oh, Sally ...

Bryan I still don't know what you're ——

Joan screams loudly, off

They all react

> *Joan stumbles into the room, distressed. She is in her dressing-gown with her make-up half-removed*

Joan (*flinging herself at Sally; frantically*) A doctor. Get a doctor.

Bryan (*startled*) What is it?

Joan (*babbling*) It's Lionel. He's had a stroke. I think he's dying. (*She sobs loudly on Sally's shoulder*)

Bryan Where is he?

Joan (*fiercely*) What's it matter? Get him a bloody doctor. (*She sobs*)

Bryan (*to Sally, worriedly*) They'd never get here in this.
Sally Try the Emergency. (*To Joan*) Shush. Shush.

Bryan hurries from the room

Pamela (*uncertainly*) Shall I take a look at him? There should be someone ...
Joan (*furiously freeing herself*) You keep your hands to yourself, you thieving bitch. If it hadn't been for you, none of this would have happened. (*With menace*) If he dies, you'll regret it till the end of your days.
Pamela (*stunned*) I beg your pardon.
Joan (*mockingly*) Look at her. Butter wouldn't melt in her mouth. (*Savagely*) Well how about a fistful of knuckles? (*She lunges at Pamela with a shriek*)

Pamela steps back. Sally grabs hold of Joan and wrestles her on to the settee

Sally (*panting*) Now that's enough. (*Firmly*) Enough. I'll not have brawling in *my* guest house.
Joan (*snarling*) No. But you'll have a bloody jewel thief, won't you?

Isobel and Pamela react

And that's all she is. (*She glowers at Pamela*)
Sally (*faintly*) Jewel thief?
Joan After her for weeks, my Lionel's been. Trailed her all the way from Sheffield. And look what good it's done him. (*She sobs*)
Sally (*to Pamela; in disbelief*) Pammy?
Pamela (*disdainfully*) She's out of her mind.
Joan (*sneering*) Don't play the innocent with me, dearie. You might have pulled wool over their eyes, but you didn't fool him for a minute. He knew what you were up to — and so do I.
Isobel (*coolly*) I think you'd better enlighten us.
Joan (*to Isobel*) Ever wondered why, when burglaries take place, the coppers never seem to find half the stuff that's been nicked? Well I'll tell you. It's because folk like her smuggle all the best bits out of the country and they're never seen again. (*She smiles nastily*) But little Miss Lightfingers, here, made a mistake. She couldn't wait to get her hands on a bit of tax-free cash, and sold a Victorian brooch to a London dealer who handed it straight back to the fella it really belonged to. And that's where Lionel came in.
Isobel (*unsteadily*) Your husband's a policeman?
Joan (*dabbing at her eyes*) Private detective. (*Glowering at Pamela*) And it didn't take him long to sniff her out.
Pamela (*to Sally; scornfully*) Believe that and you'll believe anything. (*Blustering*) For heaven's sake, Sally. I've been coming here for years.

Joan (*savagely*) And he's been after you. (*Scornfully*) Oh, but you're good, though, aren't you? Always two steps in front of him. No wonder he got depressed. If he'd swallowed any more tablets, he'd have been comatose. (*Realizing what she has said*) Oh, my God ... (*She bursts into tears again*)

Bryan enters

Bryan They're on their way, but they don't know how long it'll take them. The road's pretty bad. (*After a hesitation*) I'd better go up to him.
Joan (*snapping*) And not before time. He could be dead for all you care. (*She sobs*)

Bryan exits

Sally (*tartly*) We'll do our best for him, Mrs Reece, but we're not doctors. We don't even know we can do anything. We're as much in the dark as you are.
Pamela The medical book's by the first aid box. You could look in that.
Joan (*looking up and snapping*) We don't need your advice, thank you very much. You've done enough damage. (*She wipes at her eyes*)
Sally (*to Pamela*) It's worth a try.

Sally exits

Joan (*to Isobel*) I knew we should never have come here. I knew it. But would he listen? Not on your life. (*Bitterly*) Always knew best, did Lionel. Thought he'd catch her red-handed and go back to Sheffield like a conquering hero. "Be careful," I warned him. "If she's half as good as you say she is, she'll not let you get in her way. You're a sick man and God knows what she'd do if she found out you were on to her. " (*She sniffles*)
Isobel And how would she know that?
Joan (*irritated*) How should I know? I'm not a jewel thief. (*She glares at Pamela then glances quickly at the door*) What's he doing up there? Changing the bloody duvet covers? Why's it so quiet?
Pamela (*sitting in the armchair* L) If he has had a stroke, he might appreciate the silence. I imagine it would be quite a novelty after having you in close proximity.
Joan (*snapping*) Nobody asked for your opinion.

Sally hurries in with an open book in her hand

Sally It's not much help, but it says not to move him and not to pull on limbs if they're paralysed.

Isobel holds out her hand for the book and Sally gives it to her

(*To Joan*) And the doctors need to know if he's on medication.
Joan (*sharply*) No. (*Correcting herself*) I mean — apart from the Haloperidol.
(*She scowls at Pamela*) And he'll be off that as soon as she's behind bars.

Isobel leafs through the pages of the book

Sally (*hesitantly*) I'll give Bryan a hand. (*She moves to exit*)

Bryan enters looking serious

How is he?

Bryan shakes his head

Bryan (*to Joan*) I'm sorry.

Joan gapes at him in disbelief

Joan (*whispering*) No. (*She shrieks loudly*) Noooooooo. (*She bursts into
hysterical sobbing*)
Bryan (*helplessly*) There was nothing I could do.
Sally (*moving to Joan and sitting beside her*) We're terribly sorry, Mrs
Reece. (*Putting her arm around Joan*) Can I get you a cup of tea? It might
help ...
Joan (*roughly shrugging her off*) I don't want your bloody tea. I want Lionel.
I want my husband. (*She sobs loudly*)
Isobel (*quietly*) Had he been ill for long, Mrs Reece?
Joan (*fiercely*) He wasn't ill. He was depressed. I told you. (*She sniffles*)
Isobel But not psychotic? (*After a hesitation*) I mean — he wasn't abnormal
in any way?
Joan (*offended*) Of course he wasn't. Why should he have been?
Isobel I'm just puzzled. If he wasn't suffering from delusions — then why
was he taking Haloperidol?

Joan looks at her in bewilderment

It says here (*displaying the book*) it's a treatment for schizophrenia and the
like.
Joan (*uncertainly*) It must be a mistake.
Isobel (*surprised*) In a medical book?

Joan (*acidly*) It can happen, Ms Whatever-your-name-is. If you'd seen the things I've seen in medical books, you'd be surprised there aren't more accidental deaths. I wouldn't trust doctors as far as I could throw 'em.

Pamela You were quick enough to want one when your husband collapsed.

Joan (*snapping*) That was different. And I'll thank you to keep your nose out. (*She bursts into tears again*)

Sally comforts Joan. Bryan holds out his hand to Isobel. There are two small tablets in his palm

Bryan I suppose these must be them. I found them on the bedside carpet.

Joan (*looking up and sniffling*) He must have dropped them. Never could keep track on how many he'd taken. I'd find 'em all over the place.

Sally (*sympathetically*) That's the trouble when they're small. (*Turning her head to look at the tablets*) If you drop one, they ... (*She stops*)

Bryan (*frowning*) What?

Sally Those are Mr Tyson's pills. I'd recognize them anywhere.

Pamela You mean the ones that went missing? The what'd'you call'em things?

Sally Narfil ... Nardol. Yes.

Isobel idly checks the book index during the following

I've turned the place upside down, looking for them.

Bryan (*puzzled*) Then what were they doing in *Columbine?*

Sally looks at Joan

Joan (*defensively*) Well don't look at me. I've never seen them before. (*Frowning*) Perhaps the Pike woman ...? I mean ... She was in there before you moved us over. It could have been her who took 'em. (*She sniffles*)

Sally (*shaking her head*) She wasn't here when they vanished. She'd gone to post letters, remember?

Isobel (*unexpectedly*) Here we are. (*Reading*) "Nardil. An MOA inhibitor. Usually prescribed for clinical depression. Immediate reaction."

Bryan (*hopefully*) Are you sure he wasn't taking these instead of Haloperidol?

Joan I can read. The packet's upstairs if you want to see it. He hated tablets. He only took those because of her. (*She glares at Pamela again*)

Isobel (*reading*) "Must not be used in conjunction with other antidepressants, and users are warned to avoid cheese, red wine and chocolate whilst taking this drug to negate the risk of fatal heart attacks and strokes."

Joan (*realizing*) Oh, my God. She did it. She did it. (*Rising*) I warned him about her. I told him what would happen if she realized. (*To Pamela*) You poisoned him, didn't you? You poisoned him with those tablets.

Bryan (*hastily*) You don't know that, Mrs Reece.
Joan (*savagely to him*) Well, I didn't pinch 'em from the first aid box, did
I? I never went near it. (*She indicates Pamela*) It was her. (*Shrieking*) She
killed my husband.
Isobel (*sharply*) Did she, Mrs Reece? (*Pointedly*) Or did you do it?

All react

Joan (*gaping at Isobel in disbelief*) I beg your pardon?
Isobel You've got a blister, I believe?

Everyone looks puzzled

On your heel. You were looking for a sticking plaster, earlier.
Joan (*at a loss*) So?
Isobel When Mr Lockwood offered to get one from the first aid box, you said
there were no plasters in it and precious little else. (*Curiously*) So if you
hadn't been near it — how would you know that?
Sally (*protesting*) But there's a box of plasters in there. I got them out to use
on Derek. And what's it to do with Mr Tyson's tablets?
Pamela (*catching on*) They were there when you got the plasters — you told
me so yourself — but when I went for the Savlon, they'd gone. Which
means — while we were patching up Derek in here, she had the perfect
opportunity to slip down the hall and help herself.
Joan (*scornfully*) Don't be ridiculous. How would I know they were in
there?
Isobel You didn't. It was sheer luck, you finding them. I've no idea, of
course, why you wanted to kill him, but when you saw what the tablets
were, you realized how easily you could do it. Change his own antidepressant
for the ones you'd found, feed him with cheese sandwiches and a glass or
two of red, and Bob's your uncle. The perfect murder.
Joan (*looking at her in disbelief*) You're out of your mind. We're talking
about my husband. Not some bloody character in an Agatha Christie. How
could I know that? I can hardly tell an aspirin from a cough-drop.
(*Remembering*) And there's nothing on the bottle that says so, is there?
Isobel (*mildly*) I've no idea. I haven't seen it. (*Smiling*) But you obviously
have — or you wouldn't know there's nothing on the bottle.

Joan reacts, but quickly recovers

Joan You can argue till you're blue in the face, but I know what I know. That
bitch (*glaring at Pamela*) killed my husband, and the police'll never prove
otherwise.
Isobel Oh, I think they might. Once they know you worked in a pharmacy
at one time. (*Smiling*) Your husband mentioned it in passing.

There is a momentary silence, then Joan scowls

Joan He always *did* talk too much, the tight-fisted swine. (*Bitterly*) I hope
he rots in hell.

All react

(*Easily*) But don't get your hopes too high. Maybe I did see the bottle, after
all? Now I remember, I think I must have done. I actually wondered why
such dangerous tablets were just shoved in a first aid box that anybody
could open? You. Me. (*Indicating Bryan*) Him. Even the madman upstairs.
But we've only her word (*indicating Pamela*) somebody took 'em, haven't
we? And who's to say she didn't do it herself? After all — she had the best
motive. The minute he produced the evidence he'd found, she'd be looking
at twenty years inside. And that's the version I'll be telling the police.
(*Smiling*) Who'll do you think they'll believe? The grieving widow — or
a dykey-looking jewel thief with weight problems?
Pamela (*stung*) I may be dykey-looking, but I'm more of a human being than
you'll ever be.
Joan (*scornfully*) Spare me the homily, sweetie. You'll need all your breath
when the plods arrive. (*She moves round the back of the settee as if to exit;
then, to Bryan*) Oh — and you needn't bother making up the bill because
I've no intention of paying it. I'll be leaving with the ambulance. (*She
smiles innocently*) I'm so upset, you see, I may be in need of sedation.
Isobel (*quickly*) Aren't you forgetting something?

Joan pauses and looks at Isobel

According to this (*displays the book*) Nardil acts immediately. So Pammy
couldn't have fed it to him. She's been out in the snow for the past two
hours.
Joan (*shrugging*) That's hardly my problem. Let the police worry about it.
Isobel And if they check the bottle for fingerprints?
Joan (*pityingly*) You think I'd be that stupid?

Joan exits

Pamela subsides into the armchair

Isobel (*relieved*) Thank God for that.
Sally What?
Isobel If she's wiped her fingerprints off the bottle, she's wiped everyone
else's off, too. (*She puts the book on the radiator shelf*)
Pamela (*dispiritedly*) And how does that help?
Isobel (*patiently*) It proves that you didn't take them from the first aid box.
If you *had*, your prints'd be all over it.

Pamela And why couldn't I have wiped them off?
Isobel Because there'd be no point in doing so, then hiding the bottle in your own room. (*Nodding*) Oh, yes. That's where she's put it. I'll bet my life. It was her I heard moving about in there while you were looking for Derek. She was planting the evidence to frame you.
Sally (*rising*) We've got to call the police. (*She moves to the* R *of Bryan*)
Bryan (*to Pamela*) They're not accusing you of this.
Pamela Why should you care? Considering what I know.
Bryan Look. I know you've got some cock-eyed idea about me killing Mrs Pike, but I *didn't*. You've made a mistake. The only thing I did do was to panic. (*After a hesitation*) I was outside before dinner. It sounds stupid, I know, but the kitchen was hot, the meal was almost ready and I got this sudden urge to rush out into the snow and throw a snowball.
Sally (*staring at him*) What?
Bryan (*embarrassed*) I said it was stupid. So I slipped out of the side door, bent down to scoop some snow, and as I did so, she came round the corner. I must have frightened the life out of her when I stood up and she shot backwards, slipped, and went into the wall. I tried to grab her, but it all happened so suddenly. She cracked her head and just crumpled. I knew she was dead. I could tell it the minute I lifted her. Then I heard a noise. It must have been Derek falling into the stream ... and I panicked. I came back inside with blood on my whites and heard Lionel Reece in the dining-room. There was no way I could serve up in that state, so I slopped soup all over the bloodstains to cover them, then dashed upstairs to change. (*To Isobel*) Five minutes later, you found her.
Isobel So it was an accident, after all.
Bryan I swear it. And I don't know anything about money.
Sally (*to him*) I'll explain it all, later. (*To Pamela*) You see? He's not a murderer. I told you he couldn't be.
Pamela (*to Bryan*) I'm sorry. It all just fitted together. I should never have ... (*She rises and moves to him*) Oh, Bryan. How can you ever forgive me? (*She hugs him*)
Sally (*icily*) I'm not so sure we can. There's still the little matter of stolen jewels to explain.
Isobel (*amused*) You didn't fall for that, did you? She's not a jewel thief. You can search her luggage, if you like. The only theft she's committed was stealing a kiss from Lionel Reece under the mistletoe.

Pamela gapes at her in disbelief

(*Innocently*) I caught them at it when I first arrived. Unfortunately for them, his wife saw it, too. Told me she'd poison him before she'd let some middle-aged cow get her claws into him. Wait till the police hear that.
Sally (*surprised*) Pammy?

Sally and Bryan stare at her

Pamela (*embarrassed*) It was only the Christmas spirit. Nothing serious.
Sally (*with distaste*) I should hope so too.
Bryan But what do we do now? We can't let her go before the police arrive.

Derek enters, looking dazed. He is in pyjamas, a coverlet draped around his shoulders, his arms hanging down beneath it. His wounds have been freshly dressed and he moves unsteadily

Sally (*startled*) Derek …
Derek (*meekly*) Could I have a glass of water, please?
Sally (*hastily*) Of course you can.

Bryan quickly exits

(*Anxiously*) Are you feeling better?
Derek (*child-like*) Oh, yes. Thank you. A lot better. My head isn't hurting now.
Sally (*relieved*) I'm so glad.
Derek (*earnestly*) It was all her fault, wasn't it? That horrible Mrs Reece. She was telling lies. Mrs Pike didn't kill my mother.
Sally (*soothingly*) Of course she didn't. Mrs Pike was a very kind lady.

Sally leads Derek gently down to the settee

Derek (*satisfied*) I thought she was. I really liked her. And it was wrong of Mrs Reece to make her die, wasn't it?
Pamela Well, it wasn't really her to blame, Derek. But …
Derek (*hotly*) It was her fault. It was. If she hadn't said Mrs Pike was Caroline Faye, then Jemmy wouldn't have killed her, would he?
Pamela (*hastily*) You're right, Derek. Of course you are. But you don't have to worry about it. She won't tell any more lies, I promise …
Derek Oh, I know that. I've just made sure of it. (*With a dreamy look on his face, he produces a bloodstained kitchen knife from beneath the coverlet and gazes at it with satisfaction*)

The women react

Bryan enters with a glass of water and takes in the scene

The Lights slowly fade

CURTAIN

FURNITURE AND PROPERTY LIST

ACT I
SCENE 1

On stage: Small bookcase containing selection of paperback novels and
magazines. *On top:* ceramic bowl filled with decorated pine-cones
topped with a sprig of red-berried holly, Christmas cards
Boxed-in radiator. *On it:* small ornaments
Heavy-framed eighteenth-century oil painting or print of original
guest house building
Television set with remote control
Magazine rack containing various magazines
Long coffee table. *On it:* artificial Christmas tree, with lights, globes,
tinsel etc. *Beneath it:* gaily-wrapped boxes and packages
Ceramic bowls of hyacinths
Ornamental globes
Tall vase of holly sprigs and mistletoe
Copper or brass bowls filled with Christmas globes and tinsel
Oblong oak table
Four upright chairs
Small writing desk. *On it:* table lamp
Framed theatrical poster
Armchair
Settee to match armchair. *On arm: TVTimes*
An armchair of different design with postcards and pen on it for
Marjory
Drop-wing table with tray containing small teapot, milk jug, sugar
bowl, spoon and used cup and saucer on it
Assorted prints and paintings decorated with sprigs of holly or mistletoe
Other Christmas decorations

Off stage: Tray holding small china teapot, milk jug, sugar bowl, two cups and
saucers, two teaspoons (**Bryan**)

Personal: **Joan**: handbag containing compact and lipstick

SCENE 2

Strike: Tea things

Off stage: Glass of red wine (**Bryan**)
          Umbrella, postcards, long envelope (**Marjory**)
          Crêpe bandage, tube of ointment (**Pamela**)

ACT II
SCENE 1

Re-set: General tidy up

Strike: First aid equipment

Set: Jigsaw puzzle on table UL
          Glass of red wine for **Lionel**

Off stage: Blanket (**Isobel**)
          Umbrella sprinkled with snowflakes (**Pamela**)
          Cup of tea on a saucer (**Sally**)
          Small knapsack (**Pamela**)
          Small torch (**Bryan**)
          Small covered tray of sandwiches (**Sally**)
          Sheet of paper with family tree chart on it (**Bryan**)

SCENE 2

Strike: Tea cup, saucer and jigsaw puzzle

Off stage: Two mugs of coffee (**Bryan**)
          Small tray with two mugs of hot chocolate (**Sally**)
          Opened letter (**Pamela**)
          First aid book (**Sally**)
          Coverlet, bloodstained kitchen knife (**Derek**)
          Glass of water (**Bryan**)

Personal: **Pamela**: "snow"

LIGHTING PLOT

Practical fittings required: lighting fitment over painting, Christmas tree lights, table lamp
One interior with exterior window backing. The same throughout

ACT I, SCENE 1

To open: General dim interior lighting with dim effect on exterior backing. Christmas tree lights on

Cue 1   **Sally** flicks an unseen switch   (Page 2)
             Bring up interior lights and painting fitment to full.
             Fade exterior backing lights to black-out as scene progresses

ACT I, SCENE 2

To open: General full interior lighting with no light on exterior backing. Christmas tree lights on. Painting fitment on. Table lamp on

No cues

ACT II, SCENE 1

To open: General full interior lighting with no light on exterior backing. Christmas tree lights on. Table lamp on. Painting fitment on. Flicker effect from TV

Cue 3   **Pamela** clicks the television off   (Page 33)
             Cut flicker effect

ACT II, SCENE 2

To open: General full interior lighting with no light on exterior backing. Christmas tree lights on. Painting fitment on. Table lamp on

No cues

EFFECTS PLOT

ACT I

Cue 1   **Lionel**: "… and I'll be in the lo-lly …"   (Page 18)
           Small bell rings in hall

Cue 2   **Isobel** (*off*) "Hallo?"   (Page 19)
           Bell sounds again

ACT II

Cue 3   As ACT II begins   (Page 33)
           Dialogue and bursts of laughter from TV

Cue 4   **Pamela** clicks the television off   (Page 33)
           Cut TV sound

COPYRIGHT MUSIC

TV SOUNDTRACK